The Preparation of Teachers

An Unstudied Problem in Education

The Preparation of Teachers

An Unstudied Problem in Education

Revised Edition

Seymour B. Sarason
Kenneth S. Davidson
Burton Blatt

BROOKLINE
BOOKS
Cambridge, MA

Originally published by John Wiley and Sons, Inc.

Library of Congress Cataloging-in-Publication Data

Sarason, Seymour Bernard, 1919-
  The preparation of teachers.

  Bibliography: p.
  1. Teachers, Training of.   2. Educational psychology.
  I. Davidson, Kenneth S.   II. Blatt, Burton, 1927-
       III. Title.
LB1715.S25   1986   370'.7'1   86-4171
ISBN 0-914797-26-3

Published by
  Brookline Books, Inc.
  PO Box 1046
  Cambridge, MA 02238-1046

Printed in the United States of America at BookCrafters, Inc.

This book is dedicated
to the children and teachers
who allowed us to watch and learn

Preface to the 1986 Edition

In 1962 we knew that a book with the major thesis that
teacher education was, at best, irrelevant to classroom life and
the culture of the school and, at worst, harmful to the future
teacher, would not sit well with many people in the
educational community. Furthermore, our assertion that the
preparation of teachers was an *unstudied* problem — in the
sense of systematic study of the relationship between
preparation and the realities of the classroom *and* the school
system — seemed both unkind and unfair to generations of
theorists and researchers, let alone to those who were
responsible for preparing others for a teaching career. But
these factors received added force because the book was
published at a time when a truly lively, indeed acrimonious,
debate was raging. On one side were those who saw educators
as mushy, wooly-minded, misguided and misguiding anti-
intellectuals who had made a shambles of our schools — the
most recent example reflected in the fact that a few years
before, in 1957, we became Avis to the Russian Hertz in space.
It is hard to exaggerate the anxiety, hurt, and chagrin
engendered in most Americans by the announcement that
Russia had put a satellite in orbit. Before that event, criticism
about schools and educators had begun to mount, especially
by academics. Following the announcement, the criticisms
took on cascading proportions. And some critics indulged
their ability for satire, parody, vitriol, derogation, and
jugular-seeking ad hominems.

On the other side of the debate were those who argued that
if the quality of education had deteriorated, it was because

our society had long been niggardly in support of our schools; witness the ridiculously low salaries paid to teachers and the unwillingness to give schools vital resources (e.g., space, equipment, books, specialized personnel) to meet the different needs of children. And, these defenders queried, when will our communities, especially the urban ones, realistically confront the bewildering heterogeneity among the children in our schools? Schools, they argued, could not be judged only by what was provided by gifted or talented children, or for those of affluent parents. Did we not have an obligation to those numerous children and their parents who had experienced racial or ethnic discrimination? And what about children from families mired in poverty? And children suffering from psychological maladies, their numbers seeming to grow exponentially with each passing year? Yes, this side of the debate said, there is a lot wrong with our schools but improvement will only come when our society, so to speak, puts its money where its mouth is. They saw their opponents in debate as elitist, ignorant about schools, and basically opposed to what education in a democracy entails.

In the midst of this debate we published the first edition of *The Preparation of Teachers*, in which we stated that both sides of the debate were overlooking a problem that, if allowed to go unrecognized and unstudied, would defeat the goals and values each side espoused. It would make no difference if one side was wholly right and the other wholly wrong; if the theory and practice of teaching described two different worlds, diagnosis and prescription would be rendered ineffective. Our book could not be assimilated by either side of the debate.

But there was another factor on the scene in the early sixties — in my opinion, most fateful for our book — and that was a drastic teacher shortage. State departments of education and local school systems were either relaxing or reinterpreting requirements for teaching in order to attract more people to teaching as a career. More correctly, perhaps, they endeavored to shorten the amount of time between preservice preparation and the beginning of employment. It was not a time for reflection on or radical change in teacher preparation. And that was precisely what we called for in *The Preparation of Teachers*. It was not that we thought our book contained "the truth" or that it contained a new message. The fact is that our assertions were derivatives of what generations of teachers had said: their preparation was inadequate to the realities they faced in the classroom, the school, and the school system. And, I must emphasize, the strength and poignancy with which teachers expressed their opinions were most evident among those in our urban schools who mirrored the destabilizing transformations occurring in our metropolitan areas.

Race, ethnicity, poverty, countercultures, civil rights militancy, flight to the suburbs, the eroding tax base of our cities — these were some of the factors that, singly or in combination, made our urban areas in the early sixties stages for controversy and upset. This drama was, predictably, played out in our schools (among other places). Indeed, it was a drama that attracted to it representatives of disciplines ordinarily uninterested in schools as a site for study and consultation. It is not to impugn their motives to say that their participation was facilitated by a dramatic increase in the funds coming from a Federal government intent on improving the quality of our schools. Education was high on the national agenda and the "great educational debate" of the sixties concerned the goals and substance of education: If schools had many deficiencies, if our national health depended on a healthy school system, if we were not to repeat past errors of omission and commission, how best should we proceed?

The debate was as lively and public as it was acrimonious and ultimately fruitless. What struck us as odd at the time can be put in the form of this question: How can you spend time in or around schools and not hear teachers (especially new ones) indict the failures of their preparation? The question could have been put more generally: How can you be involved in schools, observing and dealing with staff and students, and not begin to question the relevance of the preparation of all personnel for the struggles they were experiencing?

In *The Preparation of Teachers* we focussed on teachers, but we did recognize they were not the only group whose preparation was upsettingly inadequate. We attempted to introduce the issues in the debate. The dynamics of the teacher shortage were an obstacle to taking what we described and proposed seriously. The problem facing the trainers was attracting and preparing more teachers, not overhauling their thinking and practices.

Clearly our efforts came before the thinking in the discipline was ready. In subsequent years, Burton Blatt and I continued to be involved in matters of educational policy as well as in the complex issues of institutional change. Nothing in our experience required us to alter our stance in this book. This, of course, could mean we were rigid characters, or that we were right (in large part, at least) and that future events would confirm our evaluation. Extrapolating from the past, we knew that once the debate of the sixties was over and public education was no longer on the national agenda, only a decade or so would pass before education would return to national awareness. Although you could not predict the year, or the events that would spark it, or the substantive issues that would characterize it, it was certain to return.

And, in the early eighties, it did return. Declining test scores, alarming "scientific illiteracy" among students, the difficulties of the armed forces in recruiting literate individuals, dramatically high dropout rates in our high schools, growing anxiety about the quality of the industrial sector (particularly in contrast to that of Japan), the ever-increasing gulf in educational performance between children of the "haves" and "have-nots," the perceived lack of school personnel's adherence to the maintenance of appropriate educational and behavioral standards, a sense that public schools may be intractable to change — these, together with a changing political climate, were some of the major factors that combined to catapult education back to a high position on the national agenda.

For example, when Jimmy Carter was running for President, he promised to set up a separate department of education — something long desired by the educational community. When Ronald Reagan ran for President, he proposed the elimination of that department — a proposal that seemed to arouse little negative response from society at large. Indeed, the general public seemed to agree with the criticism that schools lacked the spur of competition and had been allowed to operate like a cartel unresponsive to the needs of society. Predictably, schools and school personnel became the scapegoats for our national malaise.[1] President Reagan appointed a commission to make recommendations for "a nation at risk." Foundations got into the act, governors of many states appointed their own commissions, and hardly a week went by without a mass media story diagnosing and prescribing remedies for our educational problems. Whatever the differences among these reports, there were several points of agreement:

1. The standards by which the educational performance of students should be judged have either been ignored or allowed to deteriorate.
2. Students have either been given too much freedom to decide what courses they take or the curriculum has

---

[1] In 1983, I wrote *Schooling in America, Scapegoat and Salvation* (New York: The Free Press). One of the points I made there is that we have always viewed education as a means for personal-social-intellectual-vocational salvation at the same time that we are prepotently set to blame the schools for societal malfunctioning. The dynamics of a love-hate relationship are not conducive to dispassionate thinking and reflection, but they are mightily conducive to oversimplification and a destructive repetition compulsion.

been so watered down as to produce scientific illiteracy, and ignorance about national history and the obligations of citizenship.

3. It is an unconscionable disservice both to students and the nation to graduate those who have not met appropriate educational standards of performance.

4. A sizeable percentage of science teachers have had no formal credentials to teach science, and often even those who do possess credentials have inadequate knowledge.

5. In general, the preparation of teachers is not grounded in the liberal arts and sciences. Such a grounding is essential to fulfilling the goals of an integrated and challenging curriculum.

6. There has been a lowering of standards for admission to teacher preparation programs as well as for graduation from such programs.

7. Insufficient recognition, financial and otherwise, has been given to superior teachers.

8. The salaries of teachers should and must be raised.

My reaction to these reports has been threefold. First, they are amazingly, and I must say irresponsibly, ahistorical in that they say and recommend virtually nothing that was not articulated in the great debate of the sixties (and in debates in decades before that). The debate of the sixties gave rise to unprecedented expenditures to improve the quality of our schools. Why did these efforts fall so short of the mark? What lessons can we learn today from that failure? How do we avoid making the same mistakes about the same recommendations? The scores of commission reports leave these questions virtually unanswered.

Second, the reports are devoid of any sensitivity to what I call the culture of the school: its behavioral and programmatic regularities, the mode of and rationale for its organization, its conception of its goals, its response to internal and external sources of change, and its relationship to diverse segments of its social surround.[1] So, for example, these reports manage to avoid (quite a feat!) dealing in any meaningful, let alone direct, way with the leadership-administrative features of the school culture. Their targets are students and teachers, a targeting that betrays a profound ignorance of how the organizational and behavioral dynamics of the school culture can and do influence the climate for learning and inquiry that then influences student and teacher efforts. In short, I have argued that teaching and learning occur within a context that I refer to as the school culture. Relevant here is an excerpt from the remarks of Bruce Thomas to the Chicago United Education Committee on November 15, 1985:

> Bureaucracies require specialization that induces further rigidity and does further violence to what we know about human capacity. One of the specialized functions of bureaucracy is supervision. The dangers of supervision are clearly spelled out in some remarks by W. H. Maxwell of the New York public schools:
>
> "Principals and heads of departments do not teach classes. They are supposed to spend their whole time in supervision. There is one supervisor who does not teach for every eleven classes. In my judgment the number of non-teaching supervisors is unnecessarily large. The excessive development of supervision has resulted in several clearly defined evils in our schools.

[1] A subsequent book to this one, *The Culture of the School and the Problem of Change* (Boston: Allyn and Bacon, Second edition, 1982), initially published in 1971 indicates why the efforts of the sixties were fated to fail, and what the issues were that future efforts would have to confront. If the book has been widely read, if there has been general agreement that the issues I raised are valid and crucial, there is no evidence whatsoever that those responsible for these commission reports considered any of them. On the contrary, these reports are based on a conception of change by legislative and administrative fiat. The engineering mentality is pervasive.

"First, it has withdrawn from the work of class teaching many of our best teachers, and has thus lessened the efficiency of the teacher force as a whole.

"Second, it has created the feeling that office work and making out examination questions are more honorable than the active work of teaching....

"Third, the struggle for the prizes that are held up before the eyes of our teachers in the shape of head-of-department places, involving, as they do, in most cases, considerably less work and considerably better pay, has resulted in much unseemly wire-pulling and intrigue, an evil to be deprecated in the administration of a public-school system.

"Fourth, the multiplication of superfluous heads of departments has resulted in division of responsibility in school management, in petty jealousy, and in much harmful interference with the work of class teachers.

"Fifth, the unnecessary increase in the number of heads of departments has led to much of the excessive examination of pupils....

"Sixth, the cost of this supervision, not merely in the salaries of heads of departments, but in the fitting up of elaborate offices with expensive furniture, is withdrawing each year a vast amount of money that is sadly needed for necessary work and material."

What's interesting about these remarks is that they were written roughly 90 years ago. And what Maxwell saw at the turn of the century has only become steadily worse. Lest that seem an exaggerated statement, let me cite from Theodore Sizer's recent book on American high schools:

"Behind top-down regulation lies a distrust of American teachers. The argument is simple: the fate of an adolescent cannot be left in the hands of a semicompetent adult, however well meaning....Eventually, hierarchical bureaucracy will be totally self-validating: virtually all teachers will be semicompetent, and thus nothing but top-down control will be tolerable. American education is now well on the way to this state of affairs."

The bureaucratization of American schools, in name of systematic procedure, results only in one systematic result: structured incompetence. The result of structured incompetence is institutional pathology.

The third reaction I have had to the reports of these commissions is that what they recommend for improving the preparation of teachers has been recommended countless times in the past without discernable effect, e.g., better grounding in specific subject matter and the arts and sciences generally, better supervision, more inservice and continuing educational opportunities, stricter and more objective standards for judging teacher performance and competency, and greater and material recognition of superior teachers. It goes without saying, of course, that these recommendations are not without merit, but it is also the case that they do not speak to the question of how to prepare teachers better for the realities of the classroom, the school, and the school system. Taking courses, amassing information, acquiring unchallengeable abstractions and generalizations, learning to articulate the goals of education--these I assume hold value but it has long been obvious that learning their appropriate implementation in a classroom has not been valued. You can take scads of psychology courses and learn many valid abstractions and principles of behavior but you are still left with the applied problem of how you implement your learning in a class of 20-30 students who vary markedly in motivation, achievement, background, personality, and the degree to which they are "at risk." Much that teachers learn is derived from a psychology of *the individual*. Teachers, however, phenomenologically speaking, never deal with individuals but with *individuals in the context of a group*, an obvious fact that enormously complicates the relationship between principles and actions. Better ways to prepare teachers in this regard have not been confronted. This is why we wrote *The Preparation of Teachers* in 1962.

One writes books as much to clarify ones thinking as to state ones position for the scrutiny of a wider audience. Following the publication of this book, and as a direct result of participating in writing it, different aspects of the problem emerged and led me to formulate a proposal about the preparation of teachers. Central to my concerns was the omnipresent question: In what ways can we better prepare teachers for the realities of a career in the school culture? The observation seminar we describe in this book spoke directly to that question. But that question, I came to realize, should be seen in relation to three other questions. First, how can you make education as a field more meaningful and important for college students regardless of whether or not they seek a career in education? Second, how can education as a field in the university reduce its insularity and become more a part of the social sciences? Third, how can one address these two questions in ways that increase the size and variety of the pool of young people who seek careers in education? These questions led me to the following proposal:

1. In the undergraduate curriculum there should be a year of field experience, organized so as to expose students to major aspects of the school culture and their relationship to our society. These should not be teaching experiences, although some teaching would not be ruled out. Students would spend time in elementary, middle, and high schools. They would spend time in the superintendent's office, with principals, with special and regular education teachers, with department heads, and with the variety of people in the pupil personnel department. They would attend PTA, Board of Education, and placement team meetings. In brief, the year should be organized so as to provide observation and understanding of the school system: the different functions, roles, problems, forums, and decision-making vehicles it contains.

2. Associated with the experience — and determining its
   organization, substance, and thrust — should be a
   series of seminars, preferably on-site, each conducted
   by a representative from one of the social sciences. One
   of these seminars should, of course, be conducted by
   someone from the education faculty. The aim of each
   seminar would be to provide the student with a
   conceptual-research perspective from which to look at
   the school culture, a perspective distinctive to each of
   the social sciences and education. The observational-
   participatory experience, together with the seminars,
   should be intellectually challenging and deserving of
   full course credit. The year would be described as an
   integrated experience with school and society, not
   offered as a domain in the field of education.[1]

There would be no prerequisites for enrolling in this year.
It would be available to any undergraduate. That it would
interest those who are considering a career in education goes
without saying. But, in addition, it would interest students
majoring in any of the social sciences, if only because the year
would involve interested faculty from the social sciences.

What are some of the potential benefits that would derive
from implementing such a proposal? Those considering a

[1] When this book was written, and during the next few years when
this proposal was germinating, I had not yet read John Dewey's
1899 presidential address to the American Psychological
Association (Hilgard, E., editor, *American Psychology in Histor-
ical Perspective: Addresses of the Presidents of the American
Psychological Association, 1882-1977.* Washington, D.C.:
American Psychological Association, 1978). The title of his address
was "Psychology and Social Practice." He opens his address in this
way: "In coming before you I had hoped to deal with the problem of
the relationship of psychology to the social sciences and through
them to social practice, to life itself.... Since education is primarily
a social affair, and since educational science is first of all a social
science, we have here a section of the whole field."

career in education would be provided a realistic basis, far better than they would ordinarily have, for deciding whether such a career is appropriate for them. It could also open up education as a career option for some who never considered such a career because they never saw education as an intellectually respectable and challenging field of practice and research. In some ultimate sense, a major benefit would be the embedding of education in the mainstream of the social sciences — a goal that seeks to decrease the insularity both of the social sciences and education.

This proposal does not assume that the social sciences now possess the theories, knowledge, and methodologies for understanding the school culture, as if educators were ignoring a conceptual gold mine available to them. The social sciences have made a contribution but in a bits and pieces fashion — far less of a contribution than they can potentially make. Indeed, not only is education away from the mainstream of the social sciences, but also I know of a number of young social scientists with a strong interest in education who have been looked upon oddly by their departments because of such interests. A major obstacle to implementing my proposal is that few colleges and universities have social science departments whose members are interested in and knowledgeable about education. However, if the seriousness of this obstacle is recognized and support to overcome it is forthcoming from government and foundation sources, the obstacle could begin to be overcome. We are dealing here with both a social science and public policy issue.

I must emphasize that the thrust of this proposal, like that of *The Preparation of Teachers*, is to connect theory, research, and practice in education more intimately and productively to the realities of the school culture. I am in no way suggesting that the usual reading and discussion college course is of little or no merit to the future practitioner. But there are definite limitations and even dangers to such courses when they are not tied to observation and experience in the school culture.

In this book, we describe an observation seminar in which we and undergraduates systematically observed a "real" class over semester's time. What was so instructive about this seminar is how it concretized for the students the dilemmas and opportunities inherent in the everchanging dynamics of the classroom. No less important, it taught us, the instructors, how difficult it was for the students to become sensitive observers; to *unlearn* attitudes acquired in their years as pupils in a school classroom; to become aware that a teacher confronted with the need to act has a variety of possible responses whose consequences differ; and to understand the complexities and challenges of comprehending the different meanings of a child's behavior.

In the past several years, I have had the opportunity to interview at length teachers who had finished their teacher preparation in the previous year or two. The interviews focussed on their required courses: the substance, thrust, and relevance of these courses to their experience as new teachers. Three things clearly emerged in these interviews.

First, generally speaking, these new teachers found their required education courses to be, at best, mildly interesting but unhelpful in their experience as new teachers. They rated their subject matter courses as intellectually stimulating but clearly unhelpful in regard to teaching these subjects.

Second, a majority of these new teachers described one faculty member (never more than one) who was very helpful in that he or she assisted the student in seeing the variety of ways in which subject matter could be made interesting and appropriate for the type and level of student the teacher would have. The faculty member was described in several ways: he or she was "practical," he or she "really" knew what a classroom was like, and he or she "understood teachers and kids."

Third, little or nothing in the preparation of these new teachers helped them in thinking about and responding effectively to issues in discipline and classroom management. This, of course, is an old, old story. As one teacher put it: "Nothing in my psychology courses, and very little in my practice teaching, prepared me for the small and large problems I was faced with. I realize that there is no way to prepare a teacher so that he or she will feel completely competent in these matters when he or she is on his or her own and alone with his or her first class. But does it have to be such a baptism of fire?" And that, of course, is the fundamental question we address in this book: What is the relationship between the preparation of teachers and the realities they experience when they embark on their careers? That question is as unstudied today — as superficially discussed today — as in previous decades when the quality of education was a source of national concern.

Our emphasis in *The Preparation of Teachers* on the school culture, with a consequent deemphasis on courses, contains distinct echoes from a report that was fateful for the emergence and development of modern medicine. I refer to *The Flexner Report on Medical Education in the United States and Canada in 1910*. Several things are noteworthy in that report:

1. There were far more medical schools in 1910 than there are today.
2. Many medical schools were shoddy commercial enterprises unrelated to a university or hospital.
3. Laboratory facilities were deplorably poor. One medical school spent more on advertising than on its laboratories.
4. Entrance requirements could be as low as a couple of years of high school.

To someone accustomed to the modern medical school-medical center complexes, Flexner's report (he visited every medical school in the two countries) will come as both a surprise and a shock. But, for my present purposes, I wish to emphasize Flexner's views on acquiring knowledge and skills.

The mastery of the resources of the profession in the modern sense is conditioned upon certain definite assumptions, touching the medical student's education and intelligence. Under the apprentice system, it was not necessary to establish any such general or uniform basis. The single student was in personal contact with his preceptor. If he were young or immature, the preceptor could wait upon his development, initiating him in simple matters as they arose, postponing more difficult ones to a more propitious season; meanwhile, there were always the horses to be curried and the saddle-bags to be replenished. In the end, if the boy proved incorrigibly dull, the preceptor might ignore him till a convenient excuse discontinued the relation. During the ascendancy of the didactic school, it was indeed essential to good results that lecturers and quizmasters should be able to gauge the general level of their huge classes; but this level might well be low, and in the common absence of conscientiousness usually fell far below the allowable minimum. In any event, the student's part was, parrot-like, to absorb. His medical education consisted largely in getting by heart a prearranged system of correspondences—an array of symptoms to set off against a parallel array of doses, that, if he noticed the one, he had only to write down the other: a coated tongue—a course of calomel; a shivery back—a round of quinine. What the student did not readily apprehend could be drilled into him—towards examination time—by those who themselves recently passed through the ordeal which he was now approaching; and an efficient apparatus that spared his senses and his intellect as entirely as the drillmaster spared his industry was readily accessible at temptingly low prices in the shape of "essentials" and "quiz-compends." Thus he got, and in places still gets, his materia medica, anatomy, obstetrics, and surgery. The medical schools accepted the situation with so little reluctance that these compends were—and occasionally still are—written by the professors and sold on the premises. Under such a regime anybody could, as President Eliot remarked, "walk into a medical school from the street," and small wonder that many of those who did walk in, many "could barely read and write." (p. 21-22)

In method of instruction there is once more, nothing to distinguish medical from other sciences. Out-and-out didactic treatment is hopelessly antiquated; it belongs to an age of accepted dogma or supposedly complete information, when the professor "knew" and the students "learned." The lecture indeed continues of limited use. It may be employed in beginning a subject to orient the student, to indicate relations, to forecast a line of study in its practical bearings; from time to time, too, a lecture may profitably sum up, interpret, and relate results experimentally ascertained. Text-books, atlases, charts occupy a similar position. They are not, in the first place, a substitute for sense experience, but they may well guide and fill out the student's laboratory findings. *In general, the value of the recitation and of the quiz is in proportion to their concreteness and informality.* Outside the workshop there is danger of detachment and rote. (p. 60-61)

Flexner was an educator, and one of the preeminent ones of his day. It is interesting that his report was sponsored by the Carnegie Foundation for the Improvement of Teaching. For Flexner, the separation of theory and practice made no sense, regardless of whether it was in medicine or in education. If his report was the catalytic agent for shaping modern medicine, it was due, among other things, to his insistence on the importance of acquiring knowledge and skills in the context in which they were to be applied.[1]

It will be obvious in this book that we are not advocates of a mindless "learning by doing." We are advocates of using

---

[1] In a recent book, *Caring and Compassion in Clinical Practice* (San Francisco: Jossey-Bass, 1985), I discuss Flexner's report from the standpoint of some critical issues with which it did not deal, issues I illustrate in the fields of medicine (general medicine, and psychiatry), clinical psychology, teaching, and law. I include the preparation of teachers because I regard teaching as a clinical profession: one in which the practitioner has to deal with and help children with problems. No one, I assume, will deny that teachers daily are confronted with children troubled in one way or another, situations for which teachers are very inadequately prepared.

relevant contexts to illuminate the dilemmas and opportunities that arise when one tries to wed theory and action. It also needs to be said that there is no way to prepare teachers so that when they receive their credentials, they have, so to speak, "put it together" and need only refine what they have become. That this book does not discuss continuing education is not because we regard it as unimportant and secondary. The reports of recent years emphasize continuing education but recommend more courses be required, compounding the error of preparatory years. Not until the preparation of teachers is radically revised will the issues surrounding continuing education take on a less stultifying, self-defeating cast.

Much has happened in society and, therefore, in education since this book was first published. The rise of militant teacher unions; the passage in 1975 of Public Law 94-142 (The Education for All Handicapped Children Act); the increasing strength of the women's movement; an explosion and then a steady decline in the school-age population; declining test scores; the tendency to convert educational issues into legal ones; the setting up of a Department of Education by one president who was succeeded by another intent on dismantling it; the publication of reports critical of the Federal effort to improve education — these are only some of the factors that directly or indirectly impact our schools. Didn't the women's movement drastically change the size and characteristics of the pool of people seeking a career in teaching? Didn't Public Law 94-142 dramatically increase the variety of students with whom teachers deal? Didn't that same law explicitly seek to change the role of teachers in decision-making about individual children? Didn't stormy school-community issues require more frequent and more difficult interactions between teachers and parents? Didn't being a member of a union alter a teacher's relationship (in some way, to some degree) with administrators, the Board of Education, parents, and other teachers? The answer to these (and similar) questions is yes.

And yet, during this same period, the preparation of teachers remained unchanged. It is this kind of disjointedness between the substance of teacher training programs and the realities of schools that spurred us to write *The Preparation of Teachers* and to reissue it now. Now, as then, we concentrate on the bedrock importance of wedding theory with observation, theory with practice. The use of the verb "wedding" is not aesthetic or stylistic but is a way of emphasizing that what heretofore has been kept apart must be harmoniously joined. That wedding has yet to take place. Indeed, the direction taken by current recommendations works more toward a continued separation — in practical terms, a divorce — than a wedding.

Should the preparation of teachers be an undergraduate or a graduate experience? Should we not try to be clear about the criteria by which we will judge personal fitness for teaching? Intellectual fitness for teaching? Should we not be far less lenient than we have been about which colleges and universities should be permitted to have teacher training programs? Should we not develop a career ladder *in* teaching that is intellectually and financially rewarding so that it will attract and retain people in teaching? Should we not recognize and reward the unusually good teacher? Should it not be less difficult to dismiss poor teachers? Each of these questions is legitimate, important, and excites controversy. But, we would argue now as we did more than two decades ago, that however important these questions are, in the long run they will be unproductive for practice until the separation between theory and practice (theory and observation, theory and experience) is lessened in our teacher preparation programs. What happens to teachers once they begin their careers is, of course, of obvious importance to any effort to improve schools. We argue that such an effort will fall far short of the mark as long as the preparation of teachers continues to be *unstudied*.

This brings me to the research endeavor. One can always count on hearing that the quality of educational research must be improved, that we must attract and support young researchers, and that research findings must inform and infuse the preparation of teachers. I am not about to take a position against the academic equivalent of motherhood. Generally speaking, it is my impression that the quality of educational research has improved over the past two decades, particularly regarding the evaluation of the effects of interventions (e.g., the factors that determine whether an intervention stands a chance of achieving its goals; the relationship, often remarkably tenuous, between a stated policy and the interventions to which that policy gives rise). Ethnographic research increased noticeably in quantity and quality. Unfortunately, this research, relatively speaking, has not informed teacher preparation programs but rather seems to have had the community of researchers as its main audience. As a group, educational researchers have nothing to do with the preparation of teachers. I mean this in two ways. First, very few educational researchers have an interest in research on teacher training. Second, practically none actually and directly participates in the supervision of the student teacher. Indeed, in our prestigious universities those who are calling most articulately for upgrading programs for the preparation of teachers — and for eliminating programs substandard by their criteria — spend no part of their days in the nitty-gritty of teacher training. This, I hasten to add, does not mean that what these individuals have to say is without merit but rather, in regard to teacher training, they are incapable of seeing the gulf between theory and practice. Given their orientation, the preparation of teachers will remain unstudied. I would be delighted to be wrong.

The occasion for reissuing *The Preparation of Teachers* should be pleasurable, but in this case it is not: In January, 1985, Burton Blatt died. Anyone familiar with his professional contributions knows that Burt took the major theme of this book seriously: *You have to know and experience in the most intimate and tangible ways the situations which your actions purport to affect.* He was a teacher; and when he became a professor and then a dean of a college of education, he never forgot what it meant to be a teacher in a school and a school system. Wherever he was — Southern Connecticut State University, Boston University, Syracuse University — he influenced programs in ways consistent with what he contributed to this book. And when he became the most articulate opponent of the horrors of our residential institutions, it was not from an armchair. He not only came to know these settings but also had them photographed in the most compelling ways. But, to his everlasting credit, he did one other thing in an effort to understand how these deplorable conditions continued to exist: He became Deputy Commissioner for Mental Retardation in Massachusetts. Burt knew in an exquisite way the virtues and vices of abstract knowledge, of theories unrelated to and uninfluenced by the realities of the contexts for which they were developed. He was a man of action because through action you find out what you do not know; and why the more you know, the more you need to know. He treasured the open forum traditions of the university and he used those forums as a friendly critic of those academics who in their reverence for their theories seemed to forget that theories not only derive from real-world contexts but also can only be validated by being applied and tested in those contexts. He was a truly remarkable person and the reissue of *The Preparation of Teachers* is dedicated to his memory.

New Haven   Seymour B. Sarason
March, 1986

Foreword

The central thesis of this book is a deceptively simple one. Generally, and perhaps somewhat charitably, it is that the contents and procedures of teacher education frequently have no demonstrable relevance to the actual teaching task. The charge and the more specific diagnoses and hypotheses about improvement are likely to have a considerable and heuristic impact on programs for the preparation of teachers, if examined honestly and seriously. However, it is highly probable that this provocative little book will be ignored by those of us who need the provocation most. These preliminary remarks are written with this probability in mind.

One group of colleagues, fortunately small in number, must be dismissed from immediate consideration—those professional educators who, for reasons more personal than pedagogical, seek their secular salvation in the cult of certainty. It is another group, more heavily populated, whose attention is petitioned for in this foreword. The reader will note that the title of this volume implies criticism, and that two-thirds of the authorship resides outside the temple walls. Many of us, weary of the recent spate of "attacks," which are frequently more jaundiced than informed, have defended ourselves with a *cordon sanitaire* that is penetrated by external criticism only with great difficulty. This stance, albeit understandable, is an unfortunate one. Viewed in the cold light of objectivity, it constitutes a self-imposed restriction of the possible sources of professional information and insight.

While the foregoing characterization does not fit most teacher educators—at least at the verbal level—it cannot be dismissed lightly wherever it exists in any degree. The professional image we wish for ourselves is sharply contradicted by those who resist rather than welcome discussion of a critical nature. Indeed, there are some who strongly reject published negative treatments of education, without the courtesy of a reading, and on *ad hominem* or stereotypic grounds.

On the other hand, it is difficult to gainsay that the assumptions, methods, and curricula that define programs for preparing teachers are largely of uncertain validity. Any systematic and disinterested examination of the research relating to teacher education will suggest that strong knowledge claims are not possible. Recently, two competent investigators of the "toughminded" variety searched and appraised the published literature on the evaluation of student-teaching outcomes. They were obliged to conclude that: "Seventy years of research on teacher effectiveness have not added much to our systematic knowledge, and it is difficult to see how another seventy can do any more if the same procedures are followed."[1]

Professors Sarason, Davidson, and Blatt suggest that the teacher educator, in his search for program improvement, may be committing some of the very errors argued against. Namely, that verbalized knowledge is a sufficient condition for effective teaching behavior, and that curriculum and method can be generated on logical grounds alone, without explicit empirical reference to a clear definition of criterion behavior. The observation is a startling one, but before the teacher educator rejects it out of hand, let him ask himself when his faculty last conducted an evaluation of the preservice program against the criterion of subsequent teaching performance in terms of variables that are definitive of the

[1] Richard L. Turner and Nicholas A. Fattu, "Skill in Teaching: a Reappraisal of the Concepts and Strategies in Teacher Effectiveness Research." *Bulletin of the School of Education*, Indiana University, Vol. 36, No. 3, May 1960, p. iii.

actual teaching situation. The answer is probably an embarrassing one. Or, again, consider how frequently the criterion for curriculum improvement begins and ends with consensus or majority agreement of the faculty.

This book deserves a good hearing and a sober, critical reaction. The authors are not merely carping from the outside. Professors Sarason and Davidson, psychologists by training and inclination, conscionably participated in a teacher education program for the purpose of clarifying their views and developing the suggestive hypotheses contained in the later chapters. Professor Blatt is a Professor of Education and considers his calling a noble one. Their themes and invitations to research are not motivated by pessimism or disrespect for the task of educating prospective teachers. Rather, their book reflects a genuinely warm regard for and an informed appreciation of the teacher educator and his role.

ARTHUR P. COLADARCI
Professor of Education and Psychology
Stanford University

Preface

For a number of years, the authors of this book have been interested in and concerned with the nature and efficacy of teacher training. As colleagues on a research project on anxiety in elementary school children (Sarason, Davidson, Lighthall, Waite, and Ruebush, 1960), Drs. Sarason and Davidson found themselves becoming increasingly involved with the plight of the classroom teacher. On the one hand, they became acutely aware of the complexity of the teacher's task of guiding and stimulating children's learning and, on the other hand, of the inadequacy of their training for their difficult role. In addition, it became quite obvious that, as a group, teachers were acutely aware of this state of affairs, an awareness complicated by the knowledge that there was little they could do to remedy the situation. They could take more courses, but they held a very dim view of what they could gain thereby.

From time to time, Dr. Blatt, who, as chairman of the Department of Special Education at Southern Connecticut State College, was vitally interested in teacher training, joined in discussions with Davidson and Sarason. These discussions resulted in a more comprehensive and realistic conception of the nature and problems of teacher training and in the exploration of a new approach to teacher training at Southern Connecticut State College. This approach is described and discussed in Chapters 4 and 5 of this book.

The more we got into the problem (by talking with teachers, observing them in classrooms, and scrutinizing the contents and procedures of various teacher-training programs), the more we became convinced of two things: First, most teachers teach in a way reflecting the concept that education consists primarily of what we put into children rather than what we can get out of them. It is admittedly an exaggeration—but it may help us make our point—to say that more often than not children seem to be viewed as computers in whom we store information so that it can be recalled upon certain signals. Second, teacher-training programs reinforce this conception, that is, teachers handle children in the learning process in the same way that they were handled in the course of their professional training. These two dominant impressions are elaborated on in this book, together with recommendations about how this state of affairs can begin to be remedied.

This book has certain limitations in scope. Nowhere are we concerned with matters of curriculum (insofar as the children being taught are concerned). Also, because our own experience has been exclusively in the elementary school, our discussion draws heavily from and is most applicable to that setting. Although we believe that what we have to say is very applicable to higher grades and to those who teach there, we make no attempt to discuss such applicability.

It was our original intention to initiate and carry out systematic studies of a way of training teachers which is quite different from that reflected in present programs. Our approach, which is described in Chapters 4 and 5, could only be implemented on a very pilot basis. What with the vicissitudes of academic life (Davidson leaving Yale for Wayne State University and Blatt leaving Southern Connecticut State College for Boston University), we could not attempt more systematic studies. We felt, however, that we might make a contribution if we could formulate the problem as we saw it, a problem which has not been clearly stated or studied.

There are three people whose support and encouragement made it possible for us to look at the problem of teaching in the way we wished. We are indebted and indeed grateful to the following people: Dr. Hilton Buley, President of the Southern Connecticut State College and Dr. Charles St. Clair and Mr. Thomas Ryan, Superintendent and Assistant Superintendent, respectively, of the North Haven Schools in Connecticut. Our greatest indebtedness is to those to whom this book is dedicated.

The contents of our book reflect thinking influenced by various research projects carried out by us in many school systems over the last eight years. We wish, therefore, to express our appreciation to the following agencies who provided the necessary funds: the National Institute of Mental Health, the United States Office of Education, the Connecticut Cerebral Palsy Association, and the Office of Mental Retardation of the State of Connecticut. Finally, we wish to express our thanks to Mrs. Susan Henry for her usual excellent job of typing from a nearly illegible script.

S. B. S.
K. S. D.
B. B.

New Haven
March, 1962

Contents

1

Statement of the Problem

It would take a book of formidable size to present a comprehensive picture of what has taken place in and around our educational system over the last decade or so. We say "in and around our educational system," because it has become clearer than ever before (perhaps because it is truer now than before) that events and conditions outside physical boundaries of the school profoundly affect the processes, goals, and quality of education. We refer here to more than just the influences of sputniks and the space age on education—profound influences, to be sure, but far from being the only ones. Unprecedented population shifts (south to north, east to west, etc.), predicted but still startling population increases, the influx of various emigré groups (Puerto Rican, Cuban, Mexican), the eruption of the civil rights issue into the national consciousness—these and other developments have had no less an effect than sputniks and astronauts on what takes place in our schools.

In this book we shall be concerned with an aspect of an educational problem, the importance of which is denied by

1

nobody, but which, nevertheless, has hardly been studied. At this early point in our discussion we can state the problem as follows: What is the relevance of the contents and procedures of teacher training for the functions which a teacher performs in her or his day-by-day work? Put in another way: If one described the activities in which a teacher engages and the problems she encounters, to what extent would one find that her teacher-training experiences constitute a relevant and adequate preparation? It may come as a surprise to some that we even raise these questions, because many people assume it to be an obvious fact that teachers are trained in a way which prepares them for their job. Upon inquiry into the origins of such a surprise reaction, we generally find two views: That the primary functions of the teacher are to impart content and help in the acquisition of intellectual skills, and that teacher training prepares a prospective teacher to accomplish these objectives. In more recent years, as we shall see in subsequent chapters, there has been much criticism of conventional teacher-training programs on the basis that they have not sufficiently steeped the prospective teacher in both the scientific and liberal arts areas of knowledge. Critics see this producing poorly educated teachers who do not stimulate children to appreciate and become involved in intellectual pursuits. It should be noted that this criticism, with which we agree, assumes that the primary tasks of the teacher are to stimulate, impart knowledge to, and help children to acquire intellectual skills. To deny that these are the primary tasks of the teacher is to be for sin and against virtue. However, agreement about these primary tasks should not lull one into uncritical acceptance of the implied assumption that the accomplishment of these tasks will be a simple function of a teacher's knowledge of certain content areas (for example, the liberal arts and sciences).

It is obvious to all who have attended college that knowledge of subject matter bears no simple relationship to the effectiveness of teaching. One would have no difficulty in pointing to a host of college professors whose command of their subject matter is unquestioned but whose effectiveness in teaching is sad indeed. There are others with a similar breadth of knowledge whose effectiveness in teaching is only adequate, that is, their effectiveness in teaching does not measure up to the level of their scholarliness. There are, of course, those whose effectiveness as teachers is on the same plane as their knowledge and intellectual attainment. The frequency with which these combinations occur on the college teaching level is unknown, because it is not a problem which has been studied. Nevertheless, it seems perfectly safe to predict that when these studies are done, we shall find that expertness in a subject matter—or, for that matter, the extent of background in the liberal arts and sciences—does not guarantee effectiveness in teaching. It would seem, therefore, that in agreeing with the criticism that the training of public school teachers has tended to be deficient in depth and breadth of liberal arts and science backgrounds, it would be unfortunate, in the extreme, to assume that by rectifying this deficiency effective teaching would be assured.

By way of giving the reader some preliminary conception of the focus of this book, we shall discuss briefly certain activities and tasks of teachers and view them in terms of teacher preparatory-training. The first of these concerns a function which teachers are expected to and must perform *even though they do not receive the slightest bit of training in such a function.* We refer here to the problem of how a teacher talks with a parent. Although teachers talk to parents for diverse manifest reasons, the purpose of the talks is almost always to affect the behavior and performance of children. Some may ask why training in how to talk with parents about their children is necessary. After all, it could be argued, the aim of the teacher in talking to a parent is to inform, that is, to communicate her observations and recommendations. If the parents initiate a discussion because they have questions about their child, the teacher again has to draw upon her knowledge obtained in the classroom. In short, talking to parents about their children seems a relatively simple task which does not or should not require any special training.

There are two types of errors in the preceding argument. The first concerns a confusion between assumption and fact; that is, it is one thing to assume that talking with parents is a simple affair, and it is quite another thing to demonstrate that, in fact, parents and teachers experience their relationship as simple and straightforward, uncomplicated by matters of attitude, emotion, and conflict of interests. One would think that a function which all teachers are expected to perform would have been studied in a way so as to ascertain the effectiveness of and problems attendant to its execution. Unfortunately, this is not the case. In the absence of such studies, we can only fall back on our experiences (and those of others) based on discussion with many teachers, principals, and parents. Such experiences lead us to state that many teachers are acutely aware that their interactions with parents are far from simple, frequently unsatisfactory both to teacher and parent, and often approached on both sides with a mixture of suspicion, mistrust, and resignation. As one teacher put it, "Teachers and parents talk *to* each other far more frequently than they talk *with* each other." Needless to say, the importance of the problem stems from the fact that teacher-parent discussions so frequently concern matters which derive from or will affect the processes and goals of a child's learning and education or both.

There is a second type of error contained in the view that teachers require no special training in how to talk with parents, a type of error which we have already discussed in connection with the extent of a teacher's knowledge and its relationship to effectiveness in teaching. In the context of our present discussion we are referring to the unjustified assumption that the knowledge which a teacher has about a child—and it may be a great deal of true knowledge—ensures that it will be communicated to his parents in an effective way, that is, effective in terms of the teacher's purposes.

We started with the preceding example, which does not involve the teacher in the teaching role, in order to emphasize two points: the necessity of becoming aware of all that a teacher does, which directly or indirectly affects a child's learning, and the adequacy of her training in these respects. It is all too easy to think of a teacher as one who stands in front of a classroom instructing and guiding the learning of children. If this were anything like a true picture, then the great debate now raging in education (Chapter 2) would be robbed of much of its intensity. The fact is, as we shall try to indicate in Chapter 3, that a typical classroom day involves the teacher in a number of functions and settings other than those directly concerned with teaching, in the narrow sense of the word. The teacher, while teaching reading to one group of children, is at the same time an observer, supervisor, and disciplinarian of the other groups in the class. We cannot refrain from noting how surprised many people are when they learn that reading and other skills are rarely taught to an entire class but, rather, are handled separately in groups based on achievement level. This simple fact of classroom life immediately forces the teacher to play, simultaneously, at least two roles: teacher with one group and behavior supervisor with the other. When, as is too frequently the case, the teacher-to-be is not prepared for the pedagogical and psychological problems attendant to having several reading groups in one class, the effectiveness of the teacher and the learning of the children are affected to an undetermined degree.[1] What we are trying to empha-

---

[1] In many, if not all, methods courses in the teaching of reading, there is recognition and discussion of the necessity of different reading groups in a single room. If reactions and experiences of student teachers are used as a guide, such recognition and discussion are clearly inadequate in preparing the teacher for the management of the "real" situation. This problem will be taken up in greater detail in Chapters 4 and 5.

size here is that the nature of teacher training, its content and worth, can only be evaluated in terms of what teachers do or should be expected to do. In and of themselves, methods courses for teachers, a favorite and legitimate target of critics of teacher-training programs, are not evil things. The important question is whether such courses are relevant to the tasks confronting the teacher in the classroom. Whatever one substitutes for methods courses must be similarly evaluated.

Let us turn our attention now to an extremely important classroom function of the teacher. No one would deny that a primary aim of a teacher is to engender in children an interest in, appreciation of, and concern with the world of ideas. In the course of discussing recommendations for research on this problem, Bruner (1961, p.73) states:

> Principal among these [recommendations] were increasing the inherent interests of materials taught, giving the student a sense of discovery, translating what we have to say into the thought forms appropriate to the child, and so on. What this amounts to is developing in the child an interest in what he is learning, and with it an appropriate set of attitudes and values about intellectual activity generally. Surely we shall not by presently conceivable reforms create a nation of devoted intellectuals, nor is it apparent that this should be the major guiding aim of our schools. Rather, if teaching is done well and what we teach is worth learning, there are forces at work in our contemporary society that will provide the external prod that will get children more involved in the process of learning than they have been in the past.

For the purposes of this book, the key phrase in this quotation is "if teaching is done well," because it gives rise to a number of questions: How *do* teachers go about engendering an interest in ideas? Is the use of more interesting teaching materials capable of compensating for a teacher's lack of understanding of (or incorrect utilization of) the principles of learning and discovery? How well do teachers translate knowledge and ideas into thought forms appropriate to the child? How frequently (and we think it very frequently) is teaching conducted in a way that reflects the assumption that the aim of teaching is to "put something into the child" rather than "get something out of him?" Unfortunately, research findings, on the basis of which one might attempt to answer these questions, are lacking.

Despite the fact that these aspects of the problem are unstudied, we can turn to the question of how teachers are trained to engender an interest in the world of ideas in children. The first of two major ways of training teachers in this respect is by having them listen to lectures and read books. The prospective teacher, like all other college students, spends a lot of time in a seat in a classroom or library. We do not for a moment wish to derogate this way of learning certain things. However, the passivity with which many college students experience what is told to or read by them can work against eliciting intellectual curiosity and independence in precisely the same way that educational critics fear to be the case so frequently in the public school classroom. In any event, we can assume that under favorable circumstances much can be learned by the lecture method: Facts, ideas, and principles can be learned (on a verbal level), their interrelationships pursued and determined (on a verbal level), and a perspective in relation to an aspect of the world of ideas obtained. These are not small accomplishments. The point deserving emphasis, however, is that when facts, ideas, and principles are being learned in order to be applied to influencing the lives of others (which is the case of the teacher in relation to her pupils), the manner in which these principles are implemented may bear little relationship to their letter or spirit. It requires no research to conclude that people's actions do not always reflect the knowledge they possess or the principles they hold to be ·true.

In course lectures, discussions, and reading assignments, the prospective teacher may be "taught" about the strength of the curiosity of children, the significances of curiosity in the learning and educative process, and the different ways in which curiosity can be engendered and maintained. It does not follow that when all this knowledge is put into practice we can assume that the relation between theory and practice need be no cause of concern.

The second major way in which teachers are trained to engender an interest in the world of ideas is in the practice-teaching period. It is at this time that the prospective teacher has an opportunity to put into practice, under supervision, the knowledge obtained from college courses. In Chapters 2 and 5 we will discuss, in some detail, the aims, nature, and effectiveness of the usual practice-teaching experience. Suffice it to say, at this point, that the supervision accorded the student teacher focuses far more on the technical or engineering aspects of teaching (for example, lesson plans, special projects, curriculum materials) than on such matters as the arousal of curiosity, eliciting the contribution of the children's ideas, and the recognition of individual differences among children in terms of how this must influence the techniques of teaching. Again we turn to an excellent statement of the problem by Bruner (1961, pp. 72-73), although he does not discuss it in terms of the appropriateness of teacher training:

Somewhere between apathy and wild excitement, there is an optimum level of aroused attention that is ideal for classroom activity. What is that level? Frenzied activity fostered by the competitive project may leave no pause for reflection, for evaluation, for generalization, while excessive orderliness, with each student waiting passively for his turn, produces boredom and ultimate apathy. There is a day-to-day problem here of great significance. Short-run arousal of interest is not the same as the long-term establishment of interest in the broader sense. Films, audio-visual aids, and other such devices may have the short-run effect of catching attention. In the long run, they may produce a passive person waiting for some sort of curtain to go up to arouse him. We do not know. Perhaps anything that holds the child's attention is justified on the ground that eventually the child will develop a taste for more self-controlled attention—a point on which there is no evidence. The issue is particularly relevant in an entertainment-oriented, mass-communication culture where passivity and spectatorship are dangers. Perhaps it is in the technique of arousing attention in school that first steps can be taken to establish that active autonomy of attention that is the antithesis of the spectator's passivity.

There will always be, perhaps, mixed motives for learning among schoolchildren. There are parents and teachers to be pleased, one's contemporaries to be dealt with, one's sense of mastery to be developed. At the same time, interests are developing, the world opens up. Schoolwork is only a part of the quickened life of the growing child. To different children it means different things. To some it is the road to parental approbation; to others it is an intrusion on the social world of contemporaries, and is to be handled by the minimum effort that will get by. The culture of the school may be anti-intellectual or quite the opposite. And within this complex picture there is the subtle attraction of the subjects in school that a child finds interesting. One can spell out the details of the picture, but in the main they are familiar enough. How, within this context, do we arouse the child's interest in the world of ideas?

In our experience, the kinds of issues discussed by Bruner and the crucial question posed at the end of the quotation —it should be noted that the question and the issues concern how psychological knowledge and principles should be implemented—are rarely the prime focus of the critic teacher-student teacher relationship.

Another example illustrating the focus of this book involves one aspect of those conditions of learning facilitating the acquisition of knowledge and the utilization of one's problem-solving abilities. The aspect on which we focus here is the ability of a child to do two things: First, to be able to say "I don't know" without the admission being viewed by him or others as a sign of stupidity and, second, to be able to reflect upon and give verbal expression to his *own* ideas or methods of problem solution without undue concern about what others consider to be the "right" answer. In general, ours is not a culture in which it is easy for the individual to say "I don't know" without feeling that he is thereby inferior or will be so regarded by others. There is probably no more crucial factor in productive learning and thinking than when the recognition that one does not know or understand some-

thing is followed by the quest for knowledge and understanding. To engage in such a quest requires, particularly
in children, an interplay between internal and external
conditions, that is, the external situation (as in a classroom) can strengthen or weaken the individual's desire
to engage in the quest.

One of the unfortunate consequences of the too-frequent
inability to admit ignorance is that the individual becomes
unduly concerned with what others think and do and no
longer depends on his own intellectual resources in the
problem-solving process. If he feels that his resources are
inadequate, he becomes overly dependent on the thoughts
and productions of others. Whatever creative ideas he has
are automatically rejected and derogated, assuming that
the capacity to have a new idea has not been completely
blocked. However one defines creativity, an essential characteristic is the capacity to tolerate a new idea or conception and give it overt expression. Implied in such a characteristic is the capacity to withstand the pressure of what
is the frequent, conventional, or traditional conception.

In what ways are teachers taught how to create a psychological climate in the classroom to enable children to
appreciate and function on the basis of the principles previously discussed? Here again we find that, at best, the
prospective teacher is "told" about these principles, and
neither in the college classroom nor in the practice-teaching period is the manner in which these principles are
implemented by the student the focus of attention. As we
shall see in a later chapter, the practice-teaching period is
far more often than not conducted in a manner that pre-
vents the display of spontaneity and creativity in the student teacher. This is hardly surprising when we consider
that the emphasis in practice teaching is on matters of
curriculum content, techniques of presentation of materials,
record keeping, and, by no means rare, housekeeping.

We cannot refrain from quoting again from Bruner
(1961, pp. 67-68):

We have already noted in passing the intuitive confidence required of the poet and the literary critic in practicing their crafts: the need to proceed in the absence of specific and agreed-upon criteria for the choice of an image of the formulation of a critique. It is difficult for a teacher, a textbook, a demonstration film, to make explicit provision for the cultivation of courage in taste. As likely as not, courageous taste rests upon confidence in one's intuitions about what is moving, what is beautiful, what is tawdry. In a culture such as ours, where there is so much pressure toward uniformity of taste in our mass media of communication, so much fear of idiosyncratic style, indeed a certain suspicion of the idea of style altogether, it becomes the more important to nurture confident intuition in the realm of literature and the arts. Yet one finds a virtual vacuum of research on this topic in educational literature.

The warm praise that scientists lavish on those of their colleagues who earn the label intuitive is major evidence that intuition is a valuable commodity in science and one we should endeavor to foster in our students. The case for intuition in the arts and social studies is just as strong. But the pedagogic problems in fostering such a gift are severe and should not be overlooked in our eagerness to take the problem into the laboratory. For one thing, the intuitive method, as we have noted, often produces the wrong answer. It requires a sensitive teacher to distinguish an intuitive mistake—an interestingly wrong leap—from a stupid or ignorant mistake, and it requires a teacher who can give approval and correction simultaneously to the intuitive student. To know a subject so thoroughly that he can go easily beyond the textbook is a great deal to ask of a high school teacher. Indeed, it must happen occasionally that a student is not only more intelligent than his teacher but better informed, and develops intuitive ways of approaching problems that he cannot explain and that the teacher is simply unable to follow or recreate for himself. It is impossible for the teacher properly to reward or correct such students, and it may very well be that it is precisely our more gifted students who suffer such unrewarded effort. So along with any program for developing methods of cultivating and measuring the occurrence of intuitive thinking, there must go some practical consideration of the classroom problems and the limitations on our capacity for encouraging such skills in our students. This, too, is research that should be given all possible support.

What deserves emphasis in Bruner's statement is that consideration must be given to "classroom problems and the limitations on our capacity for encouraging such skills in our students." If, as we have done, one observes many teachers with the aim of determining the degree to which they seem able to encourage such skills in children, the picture is far from encouraging. It is the rare teacher who is both sufficiently aware of the problem *and* able to create the appropriate classroom atmosphere. Many teachers are aware of the problem and would heartily agree with all Bruner and we have said, but they are unaware of the discrepancy between the psychological principles involved and the manner in which they are implemented. However, when it is recognized that teachers have received no training in the matter, it is hardly surprising that the present picture is not a happy one.

Two factors permit us to adopt an optimistic outlook. The first is that, in our experience at least, teachers are more painfully aware than any other professional group about the inadequacies and irrelevancies of their training, particularly where the implementation of psychological principles is concerned. In these days when everyone is an expert on education, and the teacher is viewed as a semiprofessional whose objectives are clear and require no high level of ability for their successful attainment, it is hardly to be expected that teachers would proclaim, in public fashion, their awareness of the limitations of their training. Our experience with teachers (which will be taken up in Chapters 4 and 5) permits us to conclude that, as a group, they are acutely aware that their training has not adequately prepared them for the problems they encounter in the classroom. A second factor leading to an optimistic outlook is that many fields of inquiry (for example, psychology, sociology, anthropology), which have, heretofore, evinced little or no interest in education as a research area, show signs of redressing this neglect. We can only hope that, as these investigators obtain first-hand knowledge of that complex unit which goes by the name of "classroom," there will be increased recognition of the teacher as, essentially, an applied psychologist concerned with the learning process. This recognition would force attention on the inadequacies of present-day training for the role and bring the research problem of more appropriate training into focus.

In previous paragraphs we have emphasized several important aspects of the learning process, particularly curiosity and the importance of being able to be dependent on others for help in learning. How do teachers take account of these variables in teaching children? To simplify matters, let us narrow our inquiry to how teachers answer children's questions. As illustrated in Chapter 3, in our description and discussion of a classroom day, the most frequent response of teachers to a question is to answer it. What are the possible effects of *merely* answering the question? One is to reinforce the tendency to avoid using one's own capacities and knowledge for problem solving. It may be of no productive help to a child to answer his questions without determining why he is asking the question, what attempts he himself has made to answer the question, and what further possibilities he has or should consider. In other words, answering a child's question is an opportunity whereby a teacher may do far more for a child than convey information that answers the question. It is an opportunity to enable a child to become aware of the processes of learning and of *his* role in them, a kind of awareness of one's own capacities that results in productive learning, in that it increases his effectiveness with future problems. It is the rare teacher who perceives and handles children in this manner, a fact which certainly has bearing on how teachers are prepared to teach. The fact that a teacher has a class of twenty-five or more children indisputably interferes with how teachers handle questions, but it does not explain or excuse the rarity with which such handling fails to reflect awareness of the difference between feeding answers and stimulating thinking.

The last illustration in this introductory chapter stems from a discussion with a group of college juniors who had just returned from their first practice-teaching experience in an early elementary grade.

As is frequently the case with students who have just finished a practice teaching experience, the discussion quickly got around to problems of discipline. In this case the problem raised by one student concerned gum chewing. How do you stop children from chewing gum in class? The group was more than taken aback when one student said that she couldn't understand why children could not chew gum in class. After all, the student went on, children see adults chewing gum and, besides, children are always chewing or mouthing something (pencils, erasers, fingers, etc.) so why make an issue of gum chewing? One reply to this position was that you could not understand a child's speech if he had gum in his mouth. Several students (who were opposed to gum chewing) quickly retorted that most young children could talk clearly even with gum in their mouth. This discussion among the students went on for some time with apparent agreement that gum chewing was unsanitary in that children fingered the gum with their fingers, would stick it under their desk for future use, etc.

It was at this point that the instructor injected himself into the discussion: "Let us assume that gum chewing is unsanitary and that this is the reason you forbid it in the classroom. Let us also assume that you agree that children, like other human beings, like to be given explanations, particularly when you are forbidding something. What would be your explanation?"

In asking this question, the instructor was interested in determining to what extent the explanations given the children would take account of, or anticipate, the kinds of questions which would occur to children when thinking and talking about germs, illness, and contagion. Would the explanations be purely verbal? Would the teachers realize the problems children have in thinking about something they cannot see, that is, germs and viruses? Would anyone recommend that a microscope be brought to class so that the children could see that there is life invisible to the naked eye?

It should not be overlooked in the preceding example that in handling the problem of classroom rules and regulations the teacher is presented with an opportunity to stimulate children to an interest in aspects of their physical environment. However, the major reason for presenting this example was to have a basis for asking how teachers can be trained to stimulate and develop the intellectual processes and pursuits of children in what are apparently "non-academic" situations. Put in a more general way: How does one train a teacher to be so aware of a child's limitations (particularly in the realm of information) in understanding what is behind the thought processes and behavior of adults that her teaching informs as well as stimulates? We in no way wish to minimize what a teacher can learn about such principles in lectures and discussions, but we do maintain that when this is the main (if not sole) means of training teachers, it is untenable to assume that the principles will be effectively implemented. To state our position in terms of another area: The fact that someone has read about and even learned the principles underlying the conduct of psychotherapy is no basis for assuming that he will apply them appropriately.

In the pages of this chapter, we have tried to state and briefly illustrate a problem area: What is the relevance of the contents and procedures of teacher training for the functions which a teacher performs by virtue of being a content provider for, stimulant to, and supporter and overseer of the intellectual development of children? By maintaining that this is an unstudied problem, we obviously do not mean that teacher training has not been discussed. It has been discussed but, unfortunately, almost exclusively in terms of what new knowledge may be given to teachers (usually via courses) and how newly developed, instructional materials may be used. By unstudied, we mean the absence of investigations which, starting with a detailed analysis of the teacher-learner context, evaluate different approaches to teacher training in ways that permit the drawing of conclusions other than on the basis of subjective opinion. There have been too many studies in which the initial hypotheses and the final conclusions bear little or no relationship to the data collected.

A word about the scope and plan of this book. We view this book as having a limited scope, in that our focus is on the preparation of teachers as practitioners of educational psychology. More specifically, we are interested in the preparation of teachers as observers, evaluators, and influencers of the behavior and learning of children in the classroom. Even though we have a limited focus, we do not feel that we have exhausted all aspects of the problems related to it —for example, how to select teachers who will be effective practitioners of an educational psychology. We view this book primarily as an attempt to state and discuss a problem worthy of the most serious study, a problem which we feel has not been clearly stated and, therefore, not studied.

In order to gain some perspective on the preparation of teachers, it is important that this problem be viewed in the context of the controversy currently raging about our educational practices and goals. In the next chapter, we describe the contents of the debate, particularly as they affect, or may affect, the nature and goals of teacher training. In Chapter 3, we endeavor to describe a typical classroom day to illustrate how the problems a teacher must deal with and the actions she must initiate and carry through require a degree of observational skill and psychological understanding of the learning process ordinarily not obtainable in present teacher-training programs. In Chapter 4, we describe our experiences in developing a seminar designed to increase the effectiveness of teachers as observers both of themselves and their pupils in the process of learning. The role of this seminar in teacher training, its relation to traditional courses, and its implications for the conduct of the practice-teaching period are taken up in Chapter 5.

institutions seriously doubted whether elementary school teaching was anything more than a somewhat skilled occupation.

State or city agencies, recognizing a need for trained teachers, were forced to initiate these training schools, using elementary teachers and supervisors for staff. Many members of this early faculty were on a part-time basis, their major responsibilities being to the public schools. At various later points, functions never accepted by universities, insofar as teacher preparation was concerned, produced an ill-concealed contempt for training schools by these same universities. Abrogating responsibility for preparing teachers, universities "permitted" these training schools to fend for themselves. The results were disastrous, at least from the university point of view. The teacher curriculum generally consisted of "teaching under criticism" in the morning, and "mental philosophy," "method in reading and language," "method in lessons on animals," or "method in advanced lessons on plants and objects" in the afternoon. Criticism of teacher-preparation agencies produced nearly the same results fifty years ago that they are producing today. Universities began to inaugurate their own teacher-preparation programs based on a return to "standards of liberal arts schools." Normal schools began to realize that academic respectability was required before their institutions could gain acceptance, and that the critics were not entirely wrong in their insistence that teachers be as liberally educated as other so-called well-educated people. Liberal arts courses became more common in normal-school curricula.

By 1900, there were four teachers' colleges and normal schools in the country; by 1930, there were 150. A survey of these institutions during the 1940's would disclose that most of them had developed into four-year degree-granting colleges, enrolling men as well as women. It may well be that the teachers' college, the offspring of the normal school, is a temporary phenomenon in higher education

and will disappear during the lifetimes of most of our read-
ers (Miller, 1959, p. 338). Since 1951, 59 teachers' colleges
and normal schools have become state colleges and universities, and two have disappeared through mergers. The need
for this development became apparent when educators began to realize that, like law and other professions, education had been growing up from the early normal school
days of empirical application of vocational skills to a more
theoretical understanding of the profession (Brubacher,
1958, Hillberry, 1961).

During the normal school era, it was sufficient training
for would-be elementary teachers to begin work with children after several method courses in reading, arithmetic,
social studies, and student teaching, with a minimum of
liberal arts content. Secondary teachers were recruited primarily from liberal arts colleges. With the expansion of the
public secondary-school education, the consequent need for
teachers, and the increasing competencies that elementary
teachers were required to develop in our new technological
society, it became obvious that teachers needed an education that the normal school and teachers' college were not
able to provide.

There are three characteristics of the development of
teacher-training institutions which deserve emphasis. The
first is that they arose as a way of meeting a pressing social
need, that is, they did not arise to pursue theory and research in education. Second, and related to the first characteristic, the emphasis was on technical, or "practical," or
how-to-do-it matters. The third characteristic is that they
developed relatively uninfluenced by the traditions and
orientation of the universities. In the light of these characteristics, it is small wonder that, as the universities (today
as well as in earlier periods) began to be concerned with
teacher training, their criticism of ongoing practices took
two forms: derogation of the emphasis on "how to teach"
and amazement at the de-emphasis of a classical education.
It is also not surprising that the teacher-training institu-

tions tended to view such criticism as no more than what one would expect from isolates in the ivory tower. Although, in the current educational debate, there appear to be more points of contact and communication between opposing sides than was the case earlier (giving hope that what is meritorious in the criticisms of both sides will somehow be recognized), there is still a disconcerting inability on the part of many participants in the debate to view the problem in other than black and white terms. In addition, it is too often overlooked that many of the issues in the current debate are far from new and that these earlier variations may be of current significance. For example, the following quotation, written in 1893, concerned an educational issue which in substance is different from issues currently being debated but in principle is similar to them:

> The thorough-going advocates of Classics hold Latin and Greek to be indispensable to a liberal education. They do not allow of an alternative road to our University Degrees. They will not admit that the lapse of three centuries, with their numerous revolutions, and their vast development of new knowledge, makes any difference whatever to the education value of a knowledge of Greek and Roman Classics. They get over the undeniable fact that we no longer employ these languages, as language, by bringing forward a number of uses that never occurred to *Erasmus, Cassubon* or *Milton* (Bain 893, p. 359).

The specific issue which Bain spoke about appears to be resolved, but the general issue of what constitutes a sound liberal-arts background for those entering teaching remains with us.

That the issues in the current debate are far from new may be seen in some comments by Payne. Although some aspects of his statement would not be as cogent today as in 1885, his remarks could easily be taken as those of a contemporary critic, particularly those remarks bearing on "the cultivated student of learning and science."

> It cannot be said, strictly, that we have in England, at this moment, any profession of teaching. The term 'profession,' when prop-

erly, that is, technically employed, connotes or implies 'learned'; and involves the idea of an incorporated union of persons qualified by attainments and by a scientific training for a particular calling in life, and duly authorized to pursue it. It is in this sense alone that the term is employed, in speaking of the professions of law, medicine, and theology. As, however, in the case of education— and speaking particularly of secondary education—no positive attainments, no special training, no authoritative credentials whatever are demanded as professional qualifications, it is obvious that there is, strictly speaking, no profession of teaching amongst us, and that when we use the term 'profession' in this application of it, we use it in a vague, inaccurate and untechnical sense. As to attainments none whatever are required of the person who 'professes' to teach. The profound ignoramus, if sufficiently endowed with assurance, may compete for public patronage on nearly equal terms with the most cultivated student of learning and science, and may in many cases even carry off the prize; while as to training, the teacher who has severely disciplined his mind by the study of the theory of education, and carefully conformed his practice to it, scarcely stands a better chance of success than the ignorant pretender who cannot even define the term 'education'; who has no conception of the meaning of 'training'; and whose empirical self-devised methods of instruction constitute the sum total of his qualifications for the office he assumes (Payne, 1885, pp. 105-6).

Although Payne obviously took a position very similar to that of many contemporary critics of teacher training, the following statement of his indicates that he did not consider knowledge gained in the traditional college program as necessary and sufficient preparation for teaching—a somewhat unusual sense of balance.

We can have little hesitation then in asserting that the pretension to be able to teach without knowing even what teaching means; without mastering its processes and methods as an art; without gaining some acquaintance with its doctrines as a science; without studying what has been said and done by its most eminent practitioners, is an unwarrantable pretension which is so near akin to empiricism and quackery, that it is difficult to make the distinction (Payne, 1885, p. 108).

That the current debate is far from a modern phenomenon is perhaps best seen in the fact that the name of John

Dewey figures in educational controversy of decades ago as well as of today. Although certainly not alone in his efforts, John Dewey, more than any other individual, was the catalyst that triggered a controversy in education that began prior to this century and that has not abated to this date (1900, 1916, 1939). It was at the University of Chicago during the late nineteenth century that Dewey inaugurated an experimental school that tested the content of a "new pedagogy" (Blau, 1959). This early work, and his subsequent activities at Columbia University, shaped a philosophy of education that was a reaction against the classical and autocratic approach to education in vogue at the time. The "new pedagogy" concerned itself with functions that were not traditional with American public education: health, vocation, and community and family life (Cremin, 1959). In Dewey's view, all children were entitled to schooling and, therefore, both the specifics and philosophy of education needed modification. He did not believe that all children were equal in ability, but he was convinced that all could be taught, could act intelligently, to a degree, and could contribute on their own level of competence. This, for Dewey, was the purpose of education. His revolt against the proliferation of the so-called liberal or cultural courses was not a manifestation of any anti-intellectual propensities. On the contrary, Dewey was an intellectual dedicated to the scientific method both in the solution of the child's problems in school and those of his teacher and supervisor in the design of a modern everchanging curriculum. As an experimentalist, Dewey was unable to accept the rigid and stereotyped curricula, not because they were traditional or "old-fashioned," but because they did not usually lend themselves to experimental procedures—they were not always appropriate for the needs of all children. We might say that Dewey was less critical of the courses themselves than he was of methods employed to teach them. Therefore, the establishment of new courses providing direct experience, including vocational training and home arts, were the result of their amenability to the experimental concept of learning (to Dewey, experimental thinking was analogous to intelligence itself), especially for those less academically talented youngsters. However, Dewey viewed many of the more traditional offerings as vital and necessary for most children, if taught in such ways as to deliver more than empty facts to students; his preoccupation was with how, rather than what, one thinks, and he believed that children think (and learn) best when the learning is related to their experience. He viewed the dullness of *any* course as deplorable; as with Latin, vocational training did not have a special virtue in and of itself (Bruner, 1961).

Largely as a result of Dewey's work and writings, teachers began to question the practicality of certain classical courses, while classicists and other scholars became fretful over the "pedestrian how-to-do" courses being offered in schools and the quality and preparation of the teachers offering them, especially at the secondary level. Consequently, in the current educational controversy, the critics of teachers, teaching, and our schools place a large share of the blame on John Dewey—although other critics point out that the psychological principles underlying his recommended educational practices have never been adequately implemented and tested.

Some Aspects of the Current Debate

In the light of our brief sketch and discussion of the development of teacher-training institutions, it is not surprising that the so-called "Great Debate" has been described as involving "scholar" on the one side and "educationist" on the other side (Skaife, 1958).

The term "scholar" generally means an individual who is learned in one or more of the traditional fields of study. More often than not, he is a university professor, writer,

We have already noted in passing the intuitive confidence required of the poet and the literary critic in practicing their crafts: the need to proceed in the absence of specific and agreed-upon criteria for the choice of an image of the formulation of a critique. It is difficult for a teacher, a textbook, a demonstration film, to make explicit provision for the cultivation of courage in taste. As likely as not, courageous taste rests upon confidence in one's intuitions about what is moving, what is beautiful, what is tawdry. In a culture such as ours, where there is so much pressure toward uniformity of taste in our mass media of communication, so much fear of idiosyncratic style, indeed a certain suspicion of the idea of style altogether, it becomes the more important to nurture confident intuition in the realm of literature and the arts. Yet one finds a virtual vacuum of research on this topic in educational literature.

The warm praise that scientists lavish on those of their colleagues who earn the label intuitive is major evidence that intuition is a valuable commodity in science and one we should endeavor to foster in our students. The case for intuition in the arts and social studies is just as strong. But the pedagogic problems in fostering such a gift are severe and should not be overlooked in our eagerness to take the problem into the laboratory. For one thing, the intuitive method, as we have noted, often produces the wrong answer. It requires a sensitive teacher to distinguish an intuitive mistake—an interestingly wrong leap—from a stupid or ignorant mistake, and it requires a teacher who can give approval and correction simultaneously to the intuitive student. To know a subject so thoroughly that he can go easily beyond the textbook is a great deal to ask of a high school teacher. Indeed, it must happen occasionally that a student is not only more intelligent than his teacher but better informed, and develops intuitive ways of approaching problems that he cannot explain and that the teacher is simply unable to follow or recreate for himself. It is impossible for the teacher properly to reward or correct such students, and it may very well be that it is precisely our more gifted students who suffer such unrewarded effort. So along with any program for developing methods of cultivating and measuring the occurrence of intuitive thinking, there must go some practical consideration of the classroom problems and the limitations on our capacity for encouraging such skills in our students. This, too, is research that should be given all possible support.

What deserves emphasis in Bruner's statement is that consideration must be given to "classroom problems and the limitations on our capacity for encouraging such skills in

our students." If, as we have done, one observes many
teachers with the aim of determining the degree to which
they seem able to encourage such skills in children, the
picture is far from encouraging. It is the rare teacher who
is both sufficiently aware of the problem *and* able to create
the appropriate classroom atmosphere. Many teachers are
aware of the problem and would heartily agree with all
Bruner and we have said, but they are unaware of the
discrepancy between the psychological principles involved
and the manner in which they are implemented. However,
when it is recognized that teachers have received no training in the matter, it is hardly surprising that the present
picture is not a happy one.

Two factors permit us to adopt an optimistic outlook.
The first is that, in our experience at least, teachers are
more painfully aware than any other professional group
about the inadequacies and irrelevancies of their training,
particularly where the implementation of psychological
principles is concerned. In these days when everyone is
an expert on education, and the teacher is viewed as a
semiprofessional whose objectives are clear and require no
high level of ability for their successful attainment, it is
hardly to be expected that teachers would proclaim, in
public fashion, their awareness of the limitations of their
training. Our experience with teachers (which will be taken
up in Chapters 4 and 5) permits us to conclude that, as
a group, they are acutely aware that their training has not
adequately prepared them for the problems they encounter
in the classroom. A second factor leading to an optimistic
outlook is that many fields of inquiry (for example, psychology, sociology, anthropology), which have, heretofore,
evinced little or no interest in education as a research area,
show signs of redressing this neglect. We can only hope
that, as these investigators obtain first-hand knowledge of
that complex unit which goes by the name of "classroom,"
there will be increased recognition of the teacher as, essentially, an applied psychologist concerned with the learning

ously inadequate as compared with programs for European teachers that provide liberal education for its teachers equal to that of our lawyers and other professionals.

2. Comprehensive multipurpose high schools with a variety of curricula from precollege preparation to vocational training impair the development of the talented.

3. Talented youth are not being identified and, therefore, few adequate provisions are made for them in the schools.

4. Although Dewey improved what was once too autocratic a relationship between teacher and child, he did great harm to our traditional curriculum through his great influence in establishing the "Progressive Education" movement.

5. We need national standards for children as well as for teachers. Local control impedes progress in education. "Everywhere in Europe there are uniform standards for educational goals, while the running and financing of schools is generally left to local initiative." (Rickover, 1960, p. 5.)

6. The business of allowing children to choose elective subjects to be studied in high school is disturbing, permitting them to decide on programs that may negatively affect their futures.

To remedy the preceding weaknesses, Rickover suggests that the following changes are needed in our educational system: (1) homogeneous classes, (2) a return to rugged intellectual discipline in the curriculum, (3) attention to standards of excellence, and (4) an overhauling of teacher preparation programs with particular consideration given to a study of present certification laws in the various states.

Reactions to criticisms of our schools have taken a variety of forms. One segment of the profession, a minority to be sure, seems to be in agreement with the school detractors; in fact, some are more critical of the schools than the Council for Basic Education. In contrast, there are those who feel that, ". . . school folks are being snapped at now by a lot of cannibals . . ." (Hanson, 1959, p. 326). They believe that the schools are being destroyed by irresponsible critics, and teachers are being intimidated into becoming afraid of their own shadows. This group believes that the schools could improve, but that what is lost sight of is the fact that they are now much better than they have ever been before. They do not feel that they should be made to apologize for what they have done, and they are tired of being criticized. Often they regard criticism as not constructive and well-meaning.

A third group of educators tries to find some ground for mutual understanding, either through analyses of the sources of the disagreement or through objective study of the charges and countercharges. They examine, and even tend to agree with, the charges that our schools are anti-intellectual, chaotic, and not sufficiently challenging. While they too recognize these inadequacies, they tend to view them as stemming, in large part, from large and crowded classes, limited and inferior supplies, and inadequate budgets which hardly enhance a school's program (Crosby, 1954). They counter the charges of anti-intellectualism with the reiteration of the philosophy of the modern school (Kelley, 1947):

1. Knowledge is not something that can be handed down on authority.
2. Subject matter taken on authority is not necessarily educative.
3. The best way to teach is not through the setting out of subject matter in unassociated fragments.
4. Education is not preparatory to life; it is life itself.
5. Working out purposeless tasks will not necessarily produce good discipline.
6. The answer to a particular academic problem is less important than the process.

They regard today's schools as being better able to: teach the "three R's," combat the excessiveness and insidiousness of the "three D's" (drill, drudgery, and discipline), teach concepts of democracy and freedom, communicate with parents and children, deal with exceptional children, and prepare all children for purposeful living, both vocationally and socially.

They are concerned over certain obvious problems presently with us: confused or misunderstood philosophy, weaknesses in some aspects of teacher preparation, and a lessening of public confidence. However, they do not see a return to education of the nineteenth century as the salve for our ills. They believe that our schools, with all their imperfections and overcrowdedness, are better than ever before, although there is still room for improvement. The basic issue before these educators is not the degree to which we are now better than before, but the degree to which we are willing to improve and, in fact, become as good as we are able to be.

In view of the limited scope of this book, it is not indicated that we go further into the specifics of the general debate. We have endeavored to present briefly the aspects of the debate that bear most directly on the preparation of those entering the teaching profession. At this point we attempt an appraisal of those aspects in terms of the questions posed in the previous chapter.

An Appraisal of the Debate

It is somewhat surprising, to us at least, that in the current controversy, the nature of teacher training has been discussed in very general terms and has not led to a careful description and examination of the relevance of various proposals and practices to what teachers actually are confronted with and do in the course of teaching groups of children. For example, one of the most telling criticisms made of teacher-training programs is that there has been a deplorable underemphasis of the contents and traditions of the liberal arts and sciences. Stated in the bluntest terms, this criticism holds that teachers have been poorly educated. Most educationists have come to agree with this criticism and have initiated changes in the weighting given to these areas. As we indicated in the previous chapter, however, although we agree with this criticism, what evidence warrants the conclusion that strengthening the background of teachers in the liberal arts and sciences will increase their effectiveness in communicating with children or in recognizing and adapting procedures to the range of individual differences found in any classroom? If we could observe a variety of teachers coming from a variety of different teacher-training programs, would we find that the effective teachers, however defined, come only from certain types of educational backgrounds? Would there be a high relationship between teaching effectiveness and the degree of liberal arts and science background? We consider teacher training an unstudied problem precisely because these kinds of questions have not been investigated. Obviously, teacher training has been discussed at great length, and various discussants have indicated why a certain kind of "basic" liberal arts and science background would make for noticeably more effective teaching. It is our view that these recommendations have failed to come to grips with at least two problems. The first, already mentioned, is that the amount of knowledge which an individual has acquired (particularly when passively acquired in the usual college course) in no way guarantees either that it will be properly communicated or that the spirit and traditions of the liberal arts and sciences (the enduring aspects of these fields because the status of knowledge in them is constantly changing) are being effectively inculcated in our children. The value of the liberal arts and sciences lies not only in the knowledge which they contain and produce, but in the spirit of inquiry which is their hallmark. *The communication of this spirit to children is not guaranteed by the amount of knowledge the teacher (college, high school, and elementary) possesses.* If this is so, and we think it hardly debatable, then it is an aspect of teacher training which must be faced squarely by contemporary critics if their praiseworthy aim of facilitating productive learning in children is to be achieved.

The second problem which has not been faced by contemporary critics concerns the range and consequences of individual differences in the classroom. Even where there is homogeneous grouping (for example, according to intelligence or achievement) the range of individual differences is great. It is too often overlooked or not recognized that similar test scores for all the children in a classroom in no way means that the group is homogeneous in terms of patterns of abilities, interests, motivation, curiosity, and other factors which influence processes of thinking and learning, that is, the processes of acquisition and change. In criticizing teacher-effectiveness, the contemporary critic does not seem aware of how the problem of individual differences complicates the task of the teacher, a complication that anyone who has systematically observed the teaching situation would confirm. Many teachers are deficient in the recognition of and appropriate coping with these differences in learning. To expect that this deficiency will be removed by requiring teachers to have a solid background in the liberal arts and sciences is not warranted by observation or scientific evidence. If teaching were viewed primarily as the feeding of information and knowledge to children, and this is too frequently the case at all levels of schooling, the nature of individual differences would be a less thorny problem. But, because everyone is apparently agreed that the important aim is to enable children to utilize and act upon (that is, think about) knowledge in ways which expand intellectual skills, at the same time that curiosity about ideas and problems is strengthened, then the nature and range of individual differences become crucial. Not all children can be motivated in one particular way, not all children attack problems in similar ways (not all scientists go about research in the same style), not all children are equally curious, and not all children with the same test scores learn at the same pace or in the same ways. The ability to recognize and cope with such individual differences is, unfortunately, not highly related to the degree of background in the liberal arts and sciences.

Superficially, at least, the educationist has been more aware of the preceding problem. The usual teacher-training program includes psychology courses in which individual differences are taken up. The student can observe "live" classrooms, and, of course, there are the practice-teaching experience and accompanying seminars which are supposed to help the student appropriately apply theory to practice. But, as we shall see in Chapters 4, 5, and 6, the usual teacher-training program falls far short of the objective of training students as psychological observers and tacticians capable of coping effectively with individual differences. Because our criticisms of these programs are contained in later chapters, we only list them at this point:

1. The student is usually exposed to the problem of individual differences in typical lecture courses where his role is that of the passive listener and learner, a characteristic not restricted to courses in teacher-training institutions. At best, the student is exposed to facts, ideas, and theories—an exposure which we do not criticize. What we do criticize is the failure to conduct these courses in ways that would increase the possibility that the verbal knowledge acquired will be thought about and used in appropriate ways. Our criticism is *not* that these courses are of no "practical" value; it is that we have no way of knowing whether the thinking processes and skills of the student have been influenced by the knowledge given him.

2. The so-called laboratory courses and field trips in which the student observes the "real situation" are usually structured so that the student knows what he is expected to observe and think. This structuring simply does not give the student an opportunity to understand the nature of the observational process: its selectivity, relation to personal values, its complexity, and its relation to action and plan-

ning. Recognizing and coping with individual differences in children assumes that the teacher is a sophisticated observer, a term which refers to much more than noting the overt characteristics of behavior and events. In the usual teacher-training program, the observational process is rarely the focus of training in a way which suggests that it is of much consequence for the student.

3. The practice-teaching experience, which could be of paramount significance in the training of the student as a psychological observer and tactician, usually involves everything but training in problems of observation and individual differences. There are many reasons for this unfortunate situation, but one of the major ones is that the master, critic, or supervising teachers have no special qualifications for the supervisory role, that is, they are chosen because they are considered good teachers and not because they have had special training in supervision. Perhaps more to the point is that the master teacher, coming from an identical or similar training program as the student teacher, pays far more attention to matters of lesson plans and classroom housekeeping problems than to problems which are far more difficult to communicate to the student teacher.[4]

---

[4] It should be noted that in 1957, the National Council for Accreditation of Teacher Education approved for study a series of assumptions and beliefs concerning the education of teachers (Armstrong, 1957). This is in many ways an excellent statement, taking account as it does of some of the important criticisms made of teacher-training programs. There is also recognition of the need for a more meaningful integration of classroom lectures and laboratory experiences. Student teaching, the climax of the laboratory program, is viewed as being prepared for through long-term observation of and participation with children as part of the prescribed professional program. Although it is easy to agree with this view, the report is disappointing in that it details neither the current deficiencies in professional training nor the ways of remedying them. We have seen too many programs which are supposed to reflect the Council's point of view, but which are implemented in ways which merit the strong criticism they have received. The contents of Chapters 4 and 5 represent an initial attempt on our part to state and attack the problem in specific and concrete terms.

In many ways the following statement, written in 1885, bears on what we consider to be important shortcomings of both camps in the current controversy.

There can be no doubt that the teacher should have an accurate knowledge of the subject he professes to teach, and especially for this, if for no other reason—that as his proper function is to guide the process by which his pupil is to learn, it will be of the greatest advantage to him as a guide to have gone himself through the process of learning. But, then, it is very possible that although his experience has been real and personal, it may not have been conscious—that is, that he may have been too much absorbed in the process itself to take account of the natural laws of its operation. This conscious knowledge of the method by which the mind gains ideas is, in fact, a branch of Psychology, and he may not have studied that science. Nor was it necessary for his purpose, as a learner, that he should study it. But the conditions are quite altered when he becomes a teacher. He now assumes the direction of a process which is essentially not his but the learner's; for it is obvious that he can no more think for the pupil than he can eat or sleep for him. His efficient direction, then will mainly depend on his thoughtful conscious knowledge of all the conditions of the problem which he has to solve. That problem consists in getting his pupil to learn, and it is evident that he may know his subject, without knowing the best means of making his pupil know it too, which is the assumed end of all his teaching: in other words, he may be adept in his subject, but a novice in the art of teaching it. Natural tact and insight may, in many cases, rapidly suggest that knowing a subject is a very different thing from knowing how to teach it. This conclusion is indeed involved in the very conception of an art of teaching, an art which has principles, laws, and processes peculiar to itself. (Payne, 1885, p. 112).

This excellent statement contains much food for thought for those who believe that increasing the amount of a teacher's knowledge increases her ability to communicate it to children. Less obviously, perhaps, the statement contains a view of the teaching process which assumes that the teacher is an astute psychological observer and tactician.

The position we have taken about certain aspects of the current controversy will be elaborated upon in subsequent chapters. However, as a basis for these discussions, as well as for understanding our own pilot attempts in the training of teachers in the observational process, the next chapter describes a classroom day. To the reader who has not been in a position to observe a classroom, it is hoped that the contents of the next chapter will convey something of the complexity of a teacher's task.

3

A Classroom Day

One of the points we tried to make in the first two chapters was that there is a marked discrepancy between the stated aims of teacher-training programs and the manner in which these aims are implemented. Although everyone very readily agrees that the teacher must be an astute observer and psychological tactician, the procedures whereby these skills are to be obtained are either nonexistent or ineffective. As a result of intensive and extensive observations in elementary school classrooms, another kind of discrepancy became clear to us: It is one thing to talk about the training of teachers and quite another to talk about teachers' experiences and behavior once they are actually functioning in a schoolroom.

Any discussion of teacher training should involve several questions: What, after all, are the day-to-day experiences of a teacher? What relevance do these have for teacher training? How do teachers differ in their reactions to these experiences? This discussion of the experiences and behavior of teachers, therefore, will have two parts: The first will be a presentation and discussion of the events of one teacher's day; the second will examine different teachers' methods of coping with the needs and problems of children in the learning situation.

Neither of the two parts of this chapter purports to offer scientific conclusions rigorously tested. They are attempts to clarify impressions and thoughts about what happens in classrooms. With respect to the day-account of a classroom, the question can be posed: How typical is the teacher, the day, the group of children, or even the school or community? As far as specific details are concerned regarding the behavior of children and teachers, variability is so great that the question of what is typical can only remain a matter of opinion. What is typical is that the teacher meets problems and does something about them. For example, the following account mentions a child with severe asthma. Although all teachers do not meet this problem, most have one or more children with a problem of equal difficulty for the child and the teacher. In the account that follows of a day in a second grade classroom, the purpose is to describe and discuss the teacher's methods of dealing with children in the course of learning.[1]

A Day in a Second Grade Classroom

The children's seats in this bright, cheerful room are arranged in five rows of six seats facing the teacher's desk at the front of the room. At the back of the room there is a lavatory and coat rack, and along the wall there are storage cabinets with materials from several projects neatly placed on them. The far wall from the entrance is composed of windows, though the large roof-overhang keeps

[1] The reader is reminded here of a statement from the preface of this book: "Because our own experience has been exclusively in the elementary school, our discussion draws heavily from and is most applicable to that setting. Although we believe that what we have to say is very applicable to higher grades and to those who teach there, we make no attempt to discuss such applicability."

the room free of glare. Low shelves run the length of these walls and contain various kinds of paper and supplies, games and books. Other books, apparently from the library, stand on the top of these shelves with their covers facing the room. The front wall contains blackboards, above which is the alphabet in large letters in block-printed and cursive styles. The teacher's desk at the front near the windows has two house plants, there are others on the shelves and cabinet tops. The wall facing the window has a series of bulletin boards covered with some of the children's drawings and papers.

There is also a chart listing the various duties to be performed by the children. These helpers are changed daily and include the morning leader, lunch-table hosts, duster, messenger, and the names of children in charge of pencils, snacks, calendar, shelves, balls, the bathroom and the coat rack. It should be noted that the children universally regard assignments to these tasks as recognitions and not as burdens.

8:30 TO 10:00

Many of the children come to school in buses which arrive at different times so that the room fills gradually between 8:30 and 9:00. It is a Monday morning, and the teacher, an attractive smiling woman in her late twenties, has snack and lunch money to collect. This morning she also collects and tabulates "polio slips" filled out by parents and "permission slips" for a trip to the fire station later in the week. In her collection of the lunch slips, she counts the "hot lunch" children and those who bring their own, but it does not come out right because one boy does not raise his hand for either group and is not identified until the third count.

With a smile, she says, "Well now it's straight." Then she instructs the children that they are to copy the "morning news," which is written on the board, while she completes her tabulations of the money and slips she has collected. The room is very quiet and orderly, but the teacher's work takes almost a half hour. After a few minutes, some finish writing the "morning news" and she tells them to recopy it as "it will be good practice." Some do, but soon children become restless. One gets a book to read; others are talking. Soon she speaks sharply to Marie and Andrew, "Please stop talking and do your work." Very soon the children are talking again, getting noisier and noisier. After about five minutes, the teacher says, "I like the way Chris knows what to do. He got a book and is quietly reading it." Andrew and several other children look over the library books and talk but they do not follow the set example or settle down. Finally, the teacher completes her records and sends them to the office with the messenger. "Now let's see which row is ready first. I like the way Anne is sitting up nice and tall." When the class settles down, they focus their attention on the teacher and go through the salute to the flag.

"Now it's share time. Phyllis, you're the morning leader. Let's see who has nice things to share." Phyllis comes to the front of the room with some self-consciousness, but she composes herself and leads the sharing with aplomb and pleasure. Joyce, a pretty, elegantly dressed girl, has brought a book to share. This verbal, active girl, who strives to be a leader, politely shows the book and is about to sit down when the teacher encourages her to read it to the class. The book is a "guess who lives here" story which Joyce reads with great poise and sparkle, waiting for the children to guess "who lives here" each time. The children respond with delight while the teacher sits quietly smiling at their obvious enjoyment. When the story is finished, the teacher tells Phyllis and Joyce, "You did a very nice job and so did everyone else."

10:00 to 12:30

At this point, the teacher explains the children's board work which they will do at their seats while the reading groups have separate lessons at the back of the room. This class is divided according to reading ability into three groups which read different books and have different board-work assignments.

The teacher's voice is loud and clear as she explains the "Bluebirds'" paper work, the children in that group are to copy some sentences which have a pair of rhyming words and underline each pair. "Let's see what good detectives we have in this room. Some of the sentences are tricky. I tried to fool you. See if you can find the rhyming words and trick me." She adds that Friday's papers showed improvement, suggesting they were able to work better when they were not allowed to play with games or read books after finishing their work, as permitted previously. For that reason the change in the rules about games and books will remain.

Today the "Robins" and the "Larks" have the same board work, a new type of arithmetic. Previously the arithmetic had involved problems like $3 + 2 = ?$, whereas now the formula reads $3 + ? = 5$. There are ten different problems on the blackboard, and the teacher explains that this work is new. The class seems delighted, and there is a great waving of hands and eagerness to answer. Several give correct answers before the teacher calls on Dennis, whose hand was raised, and who gives the wrong answer. She gives him a concrete example, "If I had three apples, how many more would I need to have five apples?" and waits until he gives the correct response. "How many people understand how to do this?" There is a roomful of raised hands. "How many don't?" No hands go up. The hands are raised so briefly it is difficult to note whether some have not raised their hands for either question. However, the teacher does one more example anyway.

As the morning leader passes out paper, the teacher speaks to three boys and praises the work they accomplish but adds calmly, though firmly, that they should finish. These three are dreamy and make errors so they have to redo their work. The children settle down quietly and are absorbed in their tasks. The teacher works at her desk until interrupted by Robert who tells her that some children are getting drinks. The teacher orders those children to sit down and do their work, and then walks up and down the aisles looking at the children's papers. To Frank, who writes words too close together, she says, with a little annoyance, "Now look, would you like to correct a paper like that? Start that over." Frank, a tense fidgety boy, stiffens and blushes deeply, and while he starts over, his handwriting remains cramped. As she walks around with comments like, "That's better" or "That's not as good as you usually do," she corrects some and praises others with "Don't hold your pencil so tight" or "Very nice." Mostly she speaks in a soft and flat tone, but when dealing with hyperactivity, aggressiveness, or errors and behavior that have proved resistant to change, her voice shows irritation. Teresa, a plain, peaceful, but inattentive child, who has difficulty both learning and completing her work, is dreamily watching Joyce. The teacher's voice snaps, "Teresa, do your work."

The top reading group is called to the back of the room and they seem listless and inattentive. Phyllis reads and comes to a word she doesn't know and Neil says it aloud. Again in an annoyed voice, "Are you helping her?" Neil says "no" softly. The teacher says "If you say the word, I won't know if she knows it and she won't learn it." Then the teacher sounds out the word with Phyllis who looks afraid to try, but finally whispers the answer. "Very good," she is told in a matter-of-fact tone. Each child in the group reads briefly, one child so softly the teacher says, "What? Can't you speak a little louder?" On two occasions, children at seat work raise their hands to ask questions, and the teacher shakes her head "no" very firmly.

Finally, the children in the group read the following page silently. Frank, with his usual intensity, bounces his book rapidly on his knee until he is told, "Frank, stop that jiggling!" The teacher asks Phyllis a question, but she cannot answer and looks at her book. The teacher comments, "You shouldn't have to look back. You just read it," but waits while Phyllis rereads and gives the answer. When Larry, a quiet shy boy, is questioned, his eyes fill up, and very gently the teacher helps him through to the correct reply. The teacher explains the phonics page the group should work on in their seats and asks, "How many understand this page? How many don't?" She calmly answers the questions from two boys about the meaning of some pictures.

It is recess time, and the children get their wraps. Excitement is beginning to build up. Once the group is outside, the teacher forms two teams and a running game is played, much like a relay race. Judy, a frail, quiet girl who does not like these games, tells the teacher she feels too sick to play but participates after the teacher encourages her with "Oh, you'll have fun." The children wildly cheer on their teammates, and the race is very close. There are complaints that some did not run according to the rules, but the teacher ignores these and there is very little heat to the discussion. The children have a few minutes of free play, then line up to return to the room for snack time, and are in the room at 10:45.

There is great disorder as the children hang up their wraps, go to the lavatory, and mill around while the child in charge of snacks hands out the bottles of milk. Dennis complains to the teacher that Frank has wet his shirt and goes to kick him. Dennis has a severe asthmatic condition, and he is excitable, disorganized, and aggressive. The teacher allows a double standard of conduct to exist for him. The teacher intervenes and tells Frank, "It was not nice to wet Dennis' shirt," and "Why couldn't you ask him to get out of the way?" She ignores Frank's effort to protest that he did ask. Dennis kicks Frank once more before he is lured to his seat. Fifteen minutes have passed before each child has received milk and a snack. The teacher puts up a sign in colored crayon, "Happy Birthday, Teresa," the children call out "Happy Birthday," and some girls squeal "The snack is like a party." Before the snack is over one bottle falls and breaks, and the janitor is called to remove the broken glass and clean up the milk.

"Now children, let's settle down to work and be quiet." The room becomes quieter and most of the children are working as the "Bluebirds" begin their reading lesson. "Now let's see who remembers all their vowels from last week." The group then reviews a list of words designed to present the different vowels in similar words. Each child is called on to read a few sentences, and the teacher gently helps them with words they find difficult. The teacher calls out to Marie and Andrew to stop talking and do their work and if they have finished to do it again. Ralph, who keeps turning around to see Virginia's paper and ask questions, is finally told "If I see you turn around once more, I may have to send you to the first grade again." While the reading group corrects pages done individually at their seats the previous week, two boys go to get a checker game, but the teacher stops them and gives them another paper to do. The teacher goes over the next page of their reading workbook with the "Bluebirds" and asks again who does or does not understand what they are to do and again explains one of the instructions.

Before calling the third group for their reading lesson, she walks the aisles and answers questions and comments on the papers. "John, you have lovely handwriting, but take your time." "Martin, your papers are not as good as you can do." To Janet she says "That's good," and offers some suggestions for improvement. "Lucy, you could do a lot better. You're a smart girl." Lucy, bright and tomboyish, strives hard in play and sports and does papers quickly and correctly, although rather carelessly.

It is 11:45 when the third group is called for their reading lesson; this group is more restless, takes longer to get organized, and tends to make more noise. Their attention wanders to children in the class, and Teddy, who is lost in a daydream, does not know the place when he is called on. The teacher snaps her fingers, and pointing to the place, says sharply, "There." He is very sheepish but reads well after a halting start and one error with which the teacher helps him by giving him a similar word that he knows. With this group, the teacher is generally gentle when errors are made. The group then corrects a page from their reading workbook and the teacher asks, "How many got them all right?" Two children raise their hands and she says "Good. Now next time, let's do our words carefully and take our time to make sure we get them all right." Two girls say they had one wrong, but the teacher makes no comment. During this group's lessons, the rest of the children become noisy until the teacher calls out, "I like the way Teresa is working quietly." After several such efforts, she tells the children to sit and be quiet and finally ignores the talking and movement around the room as children help each other, get paper, and sharpen pencils.

By the time this group returns to their seats it is 12:15, and the teacher calls the room to order with, "I like the way Jean is sitting up nice and straight. Mary's row is all ready." The room becomes quiet, and all the children are listening. "Children, when the reading groups are having their lessons, you have to be quiet so that we can hear the children read and so that the children working on papers won't be disturbed. I am not going to keep telling you this. Too many of you have not finished your work, so after lunch, those who haven't finished will stay inside until they do. Then they can come outside to play." Dennis groans and makes an angry face, but stops when the teacher looks at him and adds, "Those who want to play outside after lunch will have to finish their work." A number of children ask questions about having to finish and all are answered gently, but firmly, with a smile.

The children are told to prepare for lunch, and there is a scraping of chairs and the noise of books being tossed in desks and a scurrying to the lavatory to wash hands. Judy goes to the teacher's desk and waits for recognition to say "Dennis took my eraser." With a sigh, the teacher retrieves the eraser from Dennis who says, with a threatening look at Judy, "I thought it was mine." At 12:25 the lines have formed and the class walks to the cafeteria.

12:30 TO 3:00

The teacher leads the class to the cafeteria. Some of the boys punch and jostle each other as they follow the girls, but the teacher does not notice until the class stops to wait its turn to enter the cafeteria. She walks back to the boys and says, "You boys know the right way to behave in line. Now I want you to stop all this foolishness." She returns to the head of the line and, in a moment, sends the hot lunch children to the line at the lunch counter. Those who bring their lunches are sent to get their milk. The teacher chats briefly with another second grade teacher before going to the cafeteria line for her lunch.

The class has three long tables in the bright modern cafeteria, and the children are noisy as they sit down, though there are no incidents or difficulties. As the cafeteria fills up with the children from other rooms in the lower grades, the noise level rises considerably. The teacher sits at one of the three tables so she can see the other two, but only has to call out once to Ernest and Charles who talk and fool around so much that they have eaten almost nothing when only a few minutes of the lunch period remain. The children eating at her table direct much of their conversation to the teacher and tell her of events at home, new toys, trips, things they have done. She responds with genuine interest to these comments, and answers a few questions from children at the other tables. When the lunch period is over, the children return their trays and bottles and wait at the corridor, and again the noise and jostling begin. One lunch-room host has to be reminded of his duties. The teacher ignores the pushing at first and, smiling, says, "Let's see how quickly we can have a nice straight line." One boy who pushes into the line is sent with an "Excuse me" to the end of the line.

At the room, children put their lunch boxes away, and several who did not finish their morning pages are told to stay in the room until they are finished. The rest of the class goes outside for a half hour of free play until 1:30. The teacher does not have playground duty today, so she is free to spend this half hour with other teachers in a small, but cheerful, comfortably furnished teachers' room.

This half hour free-play period finds some children engaged in a boisterous game of some kind of kickball. Other children from the class stand around and watch, some with great eagerness, but fearful of joining the game. In this free-play situation, especially with the teacher absent, Judy stands nervously near the door to the building by herself.

When it's time to line up, the teacher calls the class. Some of the boys are still shouting at each other, "We won," and others, "No you didn't—we won." The teacher says "All right, children, let's be quiet," several times, and they do become somewhat quiet as they return to the room. At this point, Dennis, one of the several who had not finished his work, has made a paper airplane and is running around the room with it. Dennis is gently reprimanded for not finishing his work, and the teacher sighs when he unfolds his airplane and shows her he did some of it. Two boys had peeked out of the door and scurried to their seats and now are holding their papers up to the teacher who says, "Good, I'm glad you finished your work and it looks very neat and nice."

The children mill around the water fountain, some taking long drinks or dawdling to annoy the others until the teacher calls out to hurry up or no one will be able to drink. In a couple of minutes, all are in their seats; the arithmetic lesson begins at about 1:35. The teacher says they will do the new kind of arithmetic, "But first let's see if we all know the other kind." She writes different examples of the $3 + 2 = ?$ type and calls on children. Most have hands raised, some are waving eagerly. "Robert, you know I don't call on you if you are out of your seat." Dennis waves his hand eagerly and when called on, sits in his chair, looks at the problem, then looks in his lap. Children wave and groan to be called on, but the teacher, saying, "No, give him a chance," waits and then, pointing at the numbers, restates the problem. Dennis pauses, stares at the problem, and gives the correct answer with a big sigh. "Very good, Dennis. Now we'll try some of the new kind." To many "ooh's" and groans she writes $3 + ? = 5$ on the board and says, "Who wants to try this one?" Again many waving hands, but the teacher calls on Ernest. As he gives the wrong answer, Robert, straining to be called on, lets out the right answer, for which he is reprimanded. The teacher then leads Ernest through the problem, explaining the transition from the first kind of problem to this way of stating it. The teacher goes on with these examples, stating them in concrete terms of apples and the like, in some instances, and seeking, generally, the statement, "Two, because seven plus two is nine." The children are attentive for the most part. Ralph plays with his pencil and drops it a few times before he is told, "We aren't writing now, so you can put that away."

The arithmetic lesson continues another ten minutes until 2:00.

A few minutes previous to this, Ralph goes to the bathroom and is heard crying. The teacher goes to him and he refuses to come out because he has wet his pants. To queries from the class, she responds, "Ralph isn't feeling very well." At 2:00, however, the room empties for afternoon recess, Ralph goes to the office where he is given dry clothes, and the janitor is called to the room.

As a result of this incident, the class has a shortened recess, but it is free play and quite wild because of the teacher's absence. By 2:15 they come back to the room with instructions to rest with their heads on their desks. The teacher decides to forego lessons at this point and reads a story to the class from one of the library books. Some listen with delight while she reads quietly, but expressively, for about twenty minutes, occasionally asking them questions about the story. Others fiddle with objects in their desks, their feelings of boredom or disdain evident in their expressions. At the end, the teacher asks, "Did you like the story?" and there is a chorus of "Yesses" and "Can we have a story every day?"

"All right, children. It's time to put our things away. Now remember, tomorrow afternoon we will have the big spelling test." She tells them the words they are to know and suggests they take their books home and seek help from parents or siblings. The room is noisy as the children mill around, and there seems to be no reaction to this announcement, even when the teacher asks, "Does everyone understand?" In the last fifteen minutes, the room is in a flurry of activity as children prepare to leave. The teacher works on papers at her desk, but is interrupted by a fairly constant stream of children with questions about many matters including the spelling test, assignments of the room helpers, misplaced papers or articles, and requests to help the room helpers or the teacher. Through this period, the office sends messages over the loudspeaker announcing bus departures. The children who walk are dismissed at 3:00, and the room is suddenly quiet.

The teacher goes around the room to straighten things up. She sharpens a batch of pencils which were overlooked by the child in charge of this task. Today's papers are stacked for correction later. Finally, she works on the lesson plans for the following day and prepares some special materials for the arithmetic lesson. It is close to 4:00 when she changes the names of the helpers for tomorrow. The school day is over except for the correcting of papers.

This description, although it omits many details and interactions, presents one fact clearly: A teacher's energy, attention, perceptiveness, and abilities are constantly under pressure from the demands of the complex, intense, and varied needs and feelings of the children, in this case, thirty of them, in her classroom. It is also clear that these problems are met with varying degrees of success in preventing their interference with learning. However, regardless of the many details requiring her attention, the teacher must do something, whether her decision—consciously or unconsciously made—is to ignore the problem, follow some sort of prescribed rule, or attempt to understand the reason the problem exists.

Often the teacher feels a need for a prescribed course of action in coping with a problem, and one reason for this is that she sees so many different kinds of problems. There are tense, fidgety children, dreamers, and some who pass away the class hours waiting for recesses, free play after lunch, and gym classes so they can engage in athletics. Excitable or aggressive children, by virtue of their hyperactivity, seem omnipresent, but peaceful or very quiet or shy ones can be overlooked so easily. Some are highly motivated academically, whereas some—for reasons varied and often not easily understood—do not seem motivated at all. There are children who learn or adapt almost without effort, but, for others, these processes seem torturously long and difficult. Some request help endlessly, sometimes with no apparent need, while others almost never seek assistance although they find learning a great trial.

The implications of this wide range of individual differences are complex and will be discussed further, but first let us look at two dominant impressions from the first part of the account. At the very start of the day, the teacher has the lengthy housekeeping burden of counting lunch and snack money and tabulating the "polio" and "permission" slips. The teacher did not have free time during a gym, music, or art class for this work, nor did she have a teacher's assistant, a practice that has developed in some communities. However, the lists had to be completed and turned in quickly—at least lunch and snack money had to be counted. These tasks took almost a half hour, and the children became restless and then bored, the result being that inattentiveness and flagging motivation were greater than usual.

The second impression becomes apparent in the teacher's comment to these bored children, "Recopy the morning news. It will be good practice." This is the first sign of teaching defined as pouring knowledge and skills into children presumably in line with the notion that practice makes perfect, or at least acceptable. The questions apparently unasked include: "How will the children react to copying this? Will they feel it is meaningless? Can I postpone the counting until I provide a task they will accept and regard as meaningful?" It should be clear that there is no lack of sympathy for a teacher with time-consuming housekeeping and records. However, such sympathy should not result in condoning the resolution of the housekeeping problem in a way which contributes nothing to the learning process or, worse yet, diminishes motivation and interest.

It should be apparent from this description of the reading sessions, the arithmetic lessons, and the teacher's praise and criticism of children and their work, that, although her motivation for their success is unquestionable, she focuses on their digestion of facts and acquisition of skills, often with little attention to whether the children understand the content of their lessons. Embodied and emphasized in the lessons are the questions, "Can you read this word? Do you have the knowledge that $3 + 2 = 5$? Are you able to write these words neatly and clearly?" Each of these questions is posed to determine whether or not a child has met a criterion of effectiveness, and a negative answer to any of these questions implies a failure. This teacher is aware that she must know what a child does and does not know, as shown in her reprimanding Neil for calling out the answer and preventing her learning whether Phyllis knew the word.

However, children may recall or reproduce details of lessons with little real understanding, or they may fail to do a paper, or do it poorly, because of boredom and still understand the lesson quite fully. It is also conceivable that her constant efforts to determine whether children know the right detail or answer results in such stress on being "correct" that curiosity is impaired along with free expression of ideas. We are obviously not opposed to a teacher being interested in the correct answer, but when such interest neglects the process by which the correct answer is arrived at, and the degree to which the child can utilize the answer independently for other problems, it is difficult to conclude that the child is engaged in productive learning.

The nature and extent of another problem with which teachers have to cope is perhaps not fully clear in the day-account, but it is related to what we have just discussed. The problem might be called one of attention or concentration, or possibly communication, though these terms might oversimplify the nature of the difficulty. This teacher, as all others, has had the experience of giving clear, simple instructions, only to find that able children, as well as those who learn more slowly, do not understand. Both kinds of children, right after instruction, make "senseless" errors, and the teacher receives questions, sometimes a stream of them, about points thoroughly and clearly covered moments before. These errors and "unnecessary" questions, particularly if there are many, can be trying for teachers in the first or second grade or, for that matter, in college classrooms.

Impairment of attention occurs in all children to varying degrees, and it occurs for many reasons. Teresa, the shy little girl who admired Joyce's elegant clothes and great verve, riveted her attention on Joyce repeatedly in an obvious magnification of Joyce's worth and her own lack of it. Another example is not in the day-account, but is worthy of mention because it describes a kind of confusion that occurs not infrequently. One little boy paid attention to the teacher perhaps too well. Possibly fearing he might miss something important, he kept his eyes on the teacher whenever she spoke and, after listening to several sets of instructions for the three groups, often did not recall those for his own group. Furthermore, the actions of another reading group distracted him, and he became confused about his tasks even after they had been re-explained. It will be recalled from the day-account that there were the two boys who wanted to play checkers and were prevented from doing so. The question remains whether, in their subsequent bored inattention to their work, they continued to think about the checker game they might have had. However, the rule allowing for freedom for the children to play games when they had finished their work had been cancelled, because some had abused the privilege. One can question the fairness and value of the rule change, but more at the core of the issue is why inattention occurs, and none will disagree that boredom with work can be a factor.

What we have thus far been trying to say is that the teacher in the day-account, and we do not consider her atypical, had difficulty in observing, understanding, and dealing with the learning process so that rote learning would take its deserved secondary role and the academic motivation and intellectual curiosity of her pupils would be high, resulting in productive learning. This difficulty, which so many teachers have, can affect many, if not all, the children in a classroom. The fact that children do learn—and this can be demonstrated by the increase in scores on achievement tests—is no secure basis for concluding that this learning reflects a high degree of motivation, utilization and expression of intellectual curiosity, and a foundation for independent learning. It may reflect, in our opinion, more of what has been put into children than what they have gotten out of the learning situation.

The difficulty teachers experience in perceiving, understanding, and dealing with the complexities of the learning process is perhaps most apparent when one is dealing with "problem" children. This is seen in the day-account in the different ways the teacher responds in the case of three boys, Larry, Frank, and Dennis, whose great tension interferes with their learning and effectiveness. Larry is a quiet boy whose eyes fill with tears and who becomes essentially helpless when he finds a question difficult or feels he has done or may do something wrong. In contrast, Frank's tension is expressed in continual fidgeting and bodily tension. He holds his pencil tightly clutched and, bent over his paper, writes in tiny cramped letters. Whenever he can, Frank draws pictures of airplanes shooting and bombing, whereas Larry's free time is spent quietly reading, going over his work, or lost in thought. The teacher recognizes Larry's manifest anxiety and responds supportively, especially when his helplessness is apparent. But Frank's behavior is not a plea for help, and his fidgeting is annoying, resists change, and, therefore, may be seen as aggressive, with his airplane drawings as supporting evidence. It is as if Larry's problem is seen as involving internal feelings which disturb only himself, although many children become upset when they see and hear a crying child, while Frank's problem is seen as involving overt, controllable habits which disturb the class.

The teacher was in conflict about how to assist the third boy, Dennis, a child experiencing the same feelings. Dennis, as we have seen, is a tense, excitable, aggressive child under treatment for severe asthma. The teacher at times responds to his wildness, such as running around the room, with concern about his illness, and will provide gentle controls and supportive assistance. For example, when Dennis is very upset he experiences bouts of racking coughing. The teacher attempts to avoid this by gentleness on those occasions when he is very excited, even to the point of overlooking his physical aggression to others. She is supportive when he cannot answer a question in class; however, when Dennis did not do his work, he had to stay in during free play to complete it. The problem lies in the fact that whatever method she uses. Dennis may, inexplicably it would seem, react with any of a variety of behaviors and expressions. He may be submissive or explode further; he may become very affectionate or sulk. He may complete the work he is asked to do or may sit and dream. It is only with respect to Dennis that the teacher has commented in conversations with one of the authors, "I don't know what to do with him." However, in these conversations, though relief at not being judged inadequate was apparent, the question "Why does he behave as he does?" was set aside by the teacher as too difficult to attempt to answer. Instead, she listed his problems in an expression of sympathy for Dennis, the class, and herself, with the conclusion that it would be best for all, and especially Dennis, if he were in a special class.

It is apparent that his problems are internal and disturbing to him and external and disturbing to others. As a result, her usual methods, used with Larry and Frank, seem inappropriate, and she is in conflict about how to cope with Dennis. She feels anxious about her own competence and would derogate herself were reassurance not given. However, there are many factors—including the demands on her time and energy and the nature of teacher training—that cause her to avoid objective observations of Dennis' needs, feelings, and anxiety about his own effectiveness.

What could be said in the case of all three boys is that the teacher's mode of proceeding seemed largely a function of what she was, so to speak, forced to observe, rather than a function of a dispassionate, reflective way of observing, which would allow her to discriminate between the overt behavior of a child and his covert motivation and attitude. A teacher's mode of response is a function of the way she observes children. If her observational set does not involve a critical discrimination between overt and covert factors, if the overt is given undue weight, it reduces the likelihood that the teacher's action will have other than a temporary effect on the child's behavior. For example, if a teacher observes that a child is inattentive in the learning situation and responds to that overt fact by saying "pay attention," it does not follow (particularly in the case of children who tend to be inattentive) that her response will have much effect. Inattentiveness, as we have said before, has diverse antecedents, and unless the teacher is acutely aware of this, the effectiveness of what she does is reduced. Similarly, if a teacher observes that a child does not know the answer to a question but infers incorrectly about the reason, her response (even if it means doing nothing) *may* have little or no lasting positive effect on the child's learning. Supplying the answer to some children may reinforce their dependence, while for others it may be another lost opportunity to enable them to utilize their curiosity in problem solving. As we indicated in Chapter 1, how and when one answers a child's question must be determined not only by the observation that the child is asking a question, but by factors which can only be inferred from overt behavior.

In summarizing the discussion of this account, the following points should be stressed. First, this teacher faces many problems, not the least of which are the many needs and varied personalities of the children in her class, but these problems are not more complex or serious than those faced by all teachers. Visits to many classrooms lead us to suggest that teachers must expect problems of one kind or another in most students, and that chronic or serious difficulties will usually be found in several of them.

Second, this teacher experienced varying degrees of success in preventing children's needs and emotions from interfering with their learning and development. The account also suggests that the nature and extent of her assistance to a child in stress seems determined, in part, by her value judgments about children who seem "disturbed and hurt," as compared with those who seem "disturbing and hurting."

The third major point revolves around the occurrence of two complex, interrelated problems, namely, difficulty in attention and impaired motivation. We have emphasized that neither difficulty can be removed by request or injunction; instead, the causes within the child must be understood.

Teacher Differences

With these points in mind, we can approach the second part of this chapter in an effort to explore the question of differences among teachers. The purpose, for the various reasons cited, is in no sense to derogate the teachers or their efforts but to question at least one aspect of teacher training. That aspect is the preparation of teachers to deal with children's emotions, needs, and personalities as these intrude upon the learning process.

For any who may regard differences among teachers as minimal, either in degree or implications, our classroom-observation study (Davidson and Sarason, 1961), which provided material for the day-account, also produced results suggesting that these differences are probably anything but minimal.

These results will be reviewed briefly here. First, teachers vary considerably in the effectiveness of their methods of coping with children's needs. Also, the findings indicate that a teacher rated as more effective perceives greater differences among children, and perceives them more accurately, than a teacher whose methods are seen as less effective. These findings are, and must be regarded as, tentative and descriptive in nature rather than firm, conclusive facts. In order to give fuller meaning to these findings, let us look at observers' notes comparing three teachers' methods of coping with children's dependence, attention, and motivation, as well as their methods of dealing with so-called "behavior problems." All of these categories are clearly important, as shown in the day-account; others, which could be included would broaden but not alter the picture. It should also be noted that these variables are isolated for purposes of clarification, but are, in fact, all part of a complex network of interacting needs and behaviors which teachers encounter in their students.

DEPENDENCE

It has been our view that observation of and inferences about children's dependency needs are essential to the teaching process, perhaps especially for anxious children. Children also need assistance in developing an ability to function independently, and they vary as well in that ability as in the need and the freedom to express their dependence. Accurate perception of a child's needs in these respects is clearly necessary if a teacher is to provide effective assistance. With this in mind, then, the following observation notes are presented to show the different qualities of three second-grade teachers in observing and handling pupils' dependence. The first teacher, the teacher in the day-account already presented, tends to respond in the following ways.

The teacher gives direction for four written papers in great detail. She does not ask if there are any questions, but several are freely asked and calmly answered. To one child who says, "I don't know how to make 'rhyming words,' " the teacher answers, "Do the best you can."

Here the teacher gives very complex instructions without asking if children have questions, though she answers most of those asked. The one she does not answer involves a child's grasp not of a detail, but of the very essence of the instructions. This is not to criticize the comment, "Do the best you can," for the most effective didactic response to some questions does not require giving the child the answer.

Ernest, as the room leader, is required to conduct the morning activities such as the prayer and salute to the flag. He has difficulty carrying out this routine which has been followed for several months. The teacher assists him by starting the group whenever he seems unable to do so.

Jean, usually a shy girl, waits at the teacher's side while she helps Andrew, then helps another boy, and then goes to her desk where she gives assistance to several other children. Jean waits without recognition until she finally musters enough courage to ask the teacher her question and returns to her seat. The observer adds the general note that aggressive pupils, or those who can express their needs easily, receive attention, while the teacher seemed unaware of Jean until she demanded attention.

These two examples show how the first teacher, although she gives help willingly for the most part, often does not perceive that a child needs help until he shows distress. If he is too fearful or shy to express his needs, he may face a notable lack of recognition from the teacher. While she tends to give help freely under those conditions, a number of anxious or shy children do not gain her attention and continue to have difficulty in learning, although their intellectual capacities are above average.

The second teacher frequently responds to children's dependent behavior in these ways.

In giving directions for written work, the teacher says, "Look at the the paper. I'm going to tell you *just once*," going over the directions in detail. She calls on children who seem inattentive to see if they are paying attention, and her face and voice express good-humored despair if they are not. She picks up the papers of some who are already not doing exactly as directed and shows them to the class. Then she calls a reading group, but some children working on the paper have their hands raised. She answers one with a smile, but her voice shows irritation. She reaches out and puts down one boy's hand. He asks his question anyway and receives an answer in the same tone of irritation.

A characteristically quiet girl leaves her seat to ask the teacher's help. The teacher is busy and ignores her. The girl says nothing but remains persistently at the teacher's side. Finally the teacher turns to her; the girl asks her question and is quietly answered.

The children take out their number books and Henry begins work immediately. He goes to the teacher for help, but she sends him

back and tells him to read the instructions, which are usually difficult for him to grasp. In a few minutes he brings his paper to the
teacher for help, and she answers his question and explains the task.
Several minutes later he comes for help again and is sent back to
his seat without a word.

This teacher expects and tries to get children to function
in school with a minimum of assistance. She shows an active resistance to and suppression of requests for help as
well as disapproval of such expressions of dependence. This
is not to say she does not give help, but that she seeks sufficiently effective attention and understanding by the children so that they will either not need help or will need
only a minimum. It should be noted that a considerable
number of children in this class had difficulty either in
attending to or grasping instructions, or both. Her tendency to call on inattentive children seeks to focus their
attention on the work, but her irritation with their errors
and questions seems to arouse anxiety that interferes with
their effectiveness. It is possible that her methods in this
and other respects would be less disturbing for children
who attend to and grasp instructions more effectively than
these children, but there are very few who function so well
they do not need more assistance than is provided by instructions given "only once."

In contrast to the methods of the first two teachers, the
third teacher shows the ability to perceive children's dependency needs and often anticipates their expression.

Charles is called on by Jimmy during sharing, but says he doesn't
want to come to the front of the room. The teacher permits him to
stay in his seat and relate his experiences at the Fair to her.

A girl talks with great feeling about an error made by a cafeteria
worker. To the class, the teacher says, "Yes, that was a mistake.
Sometimes I make mistakes too. That's why I tell you when you
make mistakes not to worry about it, because everyone makes them."

Donny has left the line to put something in his desk and is too shy
to assert his right to his former position in line. The teacher tells
him he may return to his place in line and he does so.

After writing one sentence, Jack brings his paper to the teacher who had been critical of his printing. She says, "Good, that shows real improvement." He is back again in a moment to ask if he should skip a line. He is told it "might be a good idea." He goes back to his seat and is up again to ask the teacher what she meant and she explains and demonstrates. In a minute he is back to ask, "Is that how you meant?" He is told "Yes" and given further encouragement.

The last example might lead many to expect that the teacher's response would encourage an unmanageable flood of dependence. Actually, she encounters fewer demands or requests for help than the other teachers, although one attempts to prevent dependent behavior and the other varies considerably in her reactions in this respect. In dealing with this need, the third teacher's effectiveness is enhanced by her ability to anticipate, note, and deal with behavior (such as inattentiveness) that impairs learning in a way that reduces the interfering effects of such behavior. As a result, the children in her room ask for help less often.

ATTENTION

With respect to inattentiveness also, the three teachers have different reaction patterns. The following examples are from the first teacher.

Although the teacher has given orders in an angry voice to settle down and pay attention to their work, the noise and disturbance in the class continue. The teacher then tries a positive approach, "I like the way Robert and Joyce are working," and the volume of noise decreases somewhat.

These children have learned that the teacher sometimes does not see to it that her orders are carried out so that, on occasion, they feel free to disregard an order as shown here. It often seems that the teacher is unaware of all the talking, or does not deal with it, until it becomes impossible to ignore the noise. Even then her methods seem inconsistent at times, and in any event the situation is hardly conducive to attention to work.

As the teacher gives directions for a paper, one boy is playing with a paper airplane. While he appears nonchalant and inattentive, he is evidently listening because occasionally he raises his hand eagerly to recite.

The teacher is aware that this boy pays attention and "allows" him some freedom as his work is in no way impaired and his motivation remains high.

With the lowest reading group, the teacher's manner is warm and patient. They seem eager but give sporadic attention. The teacher calls on a girl to read, but she doesn't know where to start. The teacher says calmly, "She lost her place again. Let's keep our place, people." The teacher indicates the place to the girl and lets her read. After reading the girl unnoticed looks dreamily out the windows.

Again the teacher shows warmth and support, though her comment, "She's lost her place again," upset the girl whose inattention after reading was not observed by the teacher. In the following example, the first teacher also does not perceive the reasons for another girl's impaired attention or, in any event, seems to deal with the problem ineffectively.

Judy is inattentive in reading, and the teacher tells her to close her book while the group learns the new words. Judy seems unable to learn during this lesson. The observer also notes that Judy is regularly pestered by Dennis and is constantly alert for his aggression, which often passes unnoticed by the teacher.

This teacher, thus, shows variability and inconsistency in perceiving the causes of inattentiveness as well as in her effectiveness in coping with it. She, as well as the second teacher, tries to "legislate" attention, although they do it in different ways. The second teacher, as in the case of dependence, also tends to show derogatory feelings for inattention as shown in the following examples.

The teacher has just finished counting the lunch money when a boy comes to hand her his. She says, "Do you know now I have to do it all over again?" in a quiet voice, but she is tight-lipped. She stares at him silently for at least ten seconds before letting him return to his seat. The observer noted that the teacher did not give a second warning or call for lunch money which the children seem to need that early in the school year.

For the first couple of months, the teacher uses the routine of having the children put their hands on their heads whenever she wants their attention.

When the teacher gives directions, she demands strict attention and challenges children who might seem to be dreaming to repeat her words.

This teacher's behavior reflects a belief that a strong expression of her feelings, an order, or ritual will solve this general problem. However, all of these approaches show that she does not grasp that the causes of inattentiveness are different for different children. This teacher takes punitive steps—which might or might not be effective, depending on the child—as shown in the preceding examples, and particularly in the following:

In the reading group, children receive marks against their names for not watching the book, for missing a word, or for not knowing when it is their turn. To increase attention, the teacher has them look for each other's mistakes. This is done as a game, although a mark is given for a mistake, even if self-corrected. When this game is played, the children read slowly, many pointing to each word and becoming upset. The children watch the teacher to see who is getting marks and a number are so intent that they do not look at their books.

In comparison with the second teacher's tendencies to misperceive or ignore children's needs and to respond punitively, the third teacher is aware that in some situations all children will be distracted and that some children require extra support.

The attention of the class is distracted by a truck fertilizing the grass outside. The teacher says, "All right, suppose we stop and have a good look." After a few minutes she says, "It will be around for quite a while and you can see it at recess," and in a few moments most are back at work. A few have to be reminded that they can "see it later" before settling down to work.

During a test, the teacher is aware that some children are becoming inattentive. She helps bring their attention to the test with calm, offhand comments like "Would you put your finger on number 15? Can you find it, Norman?" or "Are you ready, Woody? Okay," before reading the questions.

In the reading group, Norman, who has shown little motivation for school work, pays attention only part of the time and is often withdrawn. When it is his turn to read, the teacher has to show him the place. She does this without any comment and he proceeds to read in a halting, cautious manner. This is the teacher's typical reaction in this situation.

Again, with respect to the last question, many might ask whether this solves Norman's problem which was certainly persistent and difficult. Norman's problems and the teacher's methods of coping with them will be discussed later, but it can be said that many tactics were tried with little or no success. Her response to his losing his place at least has the advantage of keeping him involved, to some extent, in the learning process and the classroom activities and does not express derogation for his ineffectiveness.

MOTIVATION

A variable intimately related to attention is motivation, as shown in the following account. This set of observation notes was taken in the first teacher's room.

A boy is jumping up and down in his eagerness to recite. The teacher does not remark on this, and calls on him. He becomes excited when he makes an error, squirms, and guesses impulsively. She waits calmly, gives him time, and he finally gives the correct answer.

While with a reading group, the teacher notices a girl, an average student, going to the back of the room to get a library book. The teacher says very mildly, "Did you take your spelling book home last night?" "Yes." To the question, "Do you know all your words to get 100?" the girl is shyly silent. "I think you should be studying instead of reading a book." The girl reluctantly puts down the book, goes back to look at the spelling words for a few minutes, and then listlessly looks out the window.

Ernest has not finished his workbook assignment. While the reading group corrects their workbooks, the teacher asks about his unfinished work but does not encourage or discipline him.

The teacher encourages independent expression by relating the story to the children's experiences. She asks children how many have ever gone fishing and encourages all to relate their experiences. She listens closely and asks questions to draw them out.

This teacher again reveals inconsistency in perception and acceptance of needs and feelings. The girl getting the book was too insecure to say she knew the spelling words, and the teacher, in this instance, reinforced the girl's insecurity. While the teacher interfered with that girl's spontaneous expression, in the last example she was able to stimulate interest very effectively. However, the teacher's emphasis in this respect seems to be on learning concrete "school" lessons. As shown in the following examples, the second teacher consistently attempts to motivate children to master the concrete details of school lessons and especially to develop speed of response.

In a speed game in a reading group, two children compete against each other to see who can first say the word. The boy is excited and eager but much too slow getting the word out to be successful. He evidently knows the words, however, because later he reads the list to the teacher with only one error.

A boy, who had done almost no work until recently, does his papers quickly and goes to get blocks to play with at his desk, although for similar play yesterday the teacher had made him sit with nothing to do. Today he is given a lecture including statements that "maybe wearing a special hat" or "going to kindergarten" will make him behave and do his work better. Again his punishment is to sit idle for a long period.

A girl is bouncy and talks a little in reading group. The teacher takes away her book and has her put her head on her desk. "If you're not going to look at the book, you're not going to have a book." The girl protests and affirms her interest in reading, but the teacher is adamant.

Morning exercises are over, and the teacher is passing out papers. An exuberant boy stops her as she passes him to tell her, "Today my baby sister is one year old." The teacher stares at him and turns away without answering.

The second teacher, then, regards knowing and being able to say a word very fast as the highest kind of achievement. However, in her desire that her pupil be "all business," she disapproves of eagerness about matters not directly associated with school lessons, although, in the last example, the boy's eagerness may well be associated with his motivation for schoolwork. In two instances, the second teacher uses withdrawal of the opportunity to learn as a punishment, something which seems both unfair and illogical. One logical result of this approach would seem to be more errors and then, possibly, further withdrawal of effort from the learning process. Although that is not the only possible outcome, it is the one that occurred here. This can be compared with these notes on the third teacher's methods.

The teacher provides extra work for pupils who finish their assignments. The children who finish will have pastel chalks and special gray drawing paper for pictures about their reading topic. In her usual manner, the teacher has the children explain how they are to use these materials.

Alice expresses concern about missing arithmetic during a class tour of the kitchen and cafeteria. The teacher says, "That's the nice thing about school—we can change things around so we don't get tired of doing the same thing."

During sharing period, a boy stumbles on the words "air compression truck." The teacher helps him with the pronunciation and asks questions to bring out the meaning of these words.

A girl has written a story at home, is asked to read it to the class, and does so happily. The teacher asks her to copy it on school paper before doing her regular work. Part way through she tells the teacher her writing is too small and she wants to start over. The teacher agrees and explains how to improve the paper. The girl starts again, but suddenly goes to the teacher once more to say she'll be very late for her other papers. She is told, "That's all right. You work on your story." The child finishes both the story and her regular work.

In maintaining her pupils' motivations, this teacher is aided by her perception not only of the varied intellectual capacities and interests children possess, but also by her ability to accept their excitement or concern and to re-assure them that they do not have to worry about errors or an inadequate performance.

BEHAVIOR PROBLEMS

Thus far, in the second portion of this chapter, we have discussed differences among the three teachers with respect to their methods of handling children's dependence, in-attentiveness, and motivation. The remaining discussion in this second portion concerns the teachers' methods of cop-ing with so-called problem children. Actually, the day-account presentation dealt, at some length, with the first teacher's work with Dennis and other children experiencing difficulties. As a result, the following will describe the meth-ods of the second and then the third teacher in dealing with a child whose problems interfere with effective learning.

Henry, who is in the second teacher's room, is an active, motivated child who has great difficulty paying attention. His school work, both written and oral, is ineffective and replete with errors. However, his comments in the sharing period and in situations outside of his lessons suggest that he is able to think in a perceptive and creative manner. He is highly motivated to learn, reacts impulsively with marked dependence when he has difficulty with his work, and his failures, resulting primarily from his inattentiveness, only prod him to improve. As described previously, this teacher expresses derogation for dependence and inattentiveness, and Henry frequently had experiences like the following.

The teacher tells the pupils to draw a witch or pumpkin after finishing their work. When Henry asks about this, she says, "Oh, you won't be able to. You're not fast enough and you must finish your work first."

In the reading group, Henry is impulsive and talks out. The teacher waves her hand in his face to quiet him. Later she criticizes how he sits and how he holds his book.

Gradually, Henry's difficulty in attending increased, and his academic effectiveness decreased. His papers became messy and had to be recopied. By the end of the school year he rarely completed papers. At this point, his behavior pattern is well-described by that observed in high anxious children, in that he has difficulty attending, cares very much how effective he is, demonstrates a considerable gap between potential and achievement, and has strong needs to be dependent. Throughout, the teacher relates to him with the view that if he paid attention he would not need help, and if he controlled his impulsiveness he would not get into trouble. The difficulty is that Henry's anxiety interferes with his ability to attend, and his needs for help are difficult for him to restrain. Eventually, Henry did withhold these requests and would sit quietly, sometimes working, sometimes not, but his motivation was markedly reduced.

The third teacher had the following experiences. Norman is a dreamer, apparently unmotivated for schoolwork of any kind, who sits staring out of the window accomplishing next to nothing, bothering no one. During the first two months, this teacher used a variety of approaches. At first she would talk with him to make sure he understood the work, which he did, and to encourage him. She did not withdraw duties he liked such as messenger, and in fact related to him as with all others. That is, she showed him acceptance, respect, and fairness. Later, this changed in that she showed him clearly that she did not accept his lack of effort by requiring him to stay in during recess and free play to work on papers. This also met with practically no success or, for that matter, really anything except calm apathy. The teacher's comment when she sought psychological consultation was, "He doesn't bother me; it bothers me that I can't reach him." This is perhaps not exactly accurate, for she had begun to show irritation and anger after several weeks of intense unsuccessful effort on her part.

In the consultation about Norman she kept saying, "I don't understand why he does nothing and doesn't seem to care." In fact there was no clear explanation for this from his school experiences. But when asked could there be some other reason why he doesn't care, the teacher recalled talking with his parents and indicated that they were like that themselves. Her effort to bring them into the work she was doing with Norman was met with apathy, withdrawal, and even a lack of concern. This reminded her of other facts about his family situation. The family was large, faced economic difficulties constantly, and the children seemed forced to supervise themselves. There was a group of three older and a group of three younger siblings. In each the children were close in age and were separated by more than two years from Norman. The children in both groups tended to enter into their own activities so that Norman was most often left to himself.

When these facts came out, she said, "Well, it sounds like he feels no one cares so why should he care how well he does, but I don't see any way I can change his family— I couldn't even get them to talk to me." The teacher and the consultant agreed (1) that if no one cared, likely he would not, (2) that it was unlikely his harried parents could or would be of real assistance, (3) that, therefore, someone else would have to be the meaningful person for Norman.

At this point she said, "It sounds like it will be me

then." She and the consultant also agreed that she would likely have to repeat many times that she cared about him and about how well he was learning. When she first stated this to Norman, he looked quizzically at her. He began to do his work after a week or so, then returned to doing nothing. When he continued to hear her say that she cared how well he learned, he said in a surprised voice, "You do like me," and began working. A subsequent observer's note reads as follows: Asked to explain the words "no" and "know" Norman said, "The teacher said 'no,' but I 'know' she likes me." The rest of the year he continued to work, though there were occasional lapses, but he was able to talk these over with his teacher.

This whole account of teacher differences might well mean to some that the teacher is the sole determinant of child behavior in school. It must be recalled, however, that children arrive in school with different personalities and attend classes under different kinds of home conditions. Dennis brought his asthma, hyperexcitability, and aggressiveness to school, Henry, his anxiety, impulsiveness, and difficulty in attending, and Norman, his apathy and withdrawal.

The descriptions should not suggest that the third teacher is somehow perfect, for some of her students still had interfering problems, or that the other teachers could not be effective, for some of their pupils responded to their methods with considerable effectiveness. However, it should be clear that teachers face, in addition to their manifold academic and housekeeping duties, the complex and varied personalities of about thirty children. In combination, these present a formidable task, requiring great time and energy from teachers. The descriptions show that teachers define their task differently, observe and understand children's needs and behavior with varying degrees of accuracy, and handle the learning situation in divergent ways.

Perhaps the most important conclusion we could state on the basis of the contents of this chapter is that the teacher must be viewed as a kind of psychological observer and tactician in a learning situation structured so that children are able to absorb and utilize knowledge and skills in an increasingly independent, curiosity-satisfying, productive attack on the world of ideas and problems. To the extent that the teacher perceives of her role as involving the input of knowledge, with little or no attention to the covert processes of learning, she is performing as a technician. Unfortunately, many teachers do not possess sophistication in observation, they tend to be uncritical of the processes by which they go from observation to action, and they are unaware of the discrepancy between theory and practice. This is not at all surprising, as was indicated at the close of the last chapter, when one realizes that the training of teachers ill prepares them for the role of psychological observer and tactician. As we shall see in the next two chapters, our criticisms of present-day teaching reflect the fact that teachers teach children in much the same way that they were taught in their professional training.

4

The Teacher as
Observer:

A Description of an
Observational Seminar

In the previous chapters of this book we have endeavored, in different ways and from varying vantage points, to indicate certain unstudied aspects of the adequacy of teacher training. Essentially, we have advanced two contentions. First, although we agree with those who feel that the teacher's knowledge and grasp of subject matter in the sciences and liberal arts have not been adequate, we feel that it would be a mistake to assume that rectifying this inadequacy insures that children will be more effectively taught, that is, become more interested in the world of ideas, more aware of and secure in their powers of discovery, and more motivated to face and master a variety of developmental problems. The learned or scholarly teacher—regardless of the age of the pupils being taught—is not necessarily the effective teacher.

The second of our major contentions was that the training of teachers in the techniques of teaching falls far short
of the goal of harmonizing educational theory and practice.
The conventional methods courses as well as the manner
of handling the practice-teaching experience too often do
not prepare the teacher to be an astute, dispassionate observer who can adapt her behavior and techniques to the
needs and capabilities of her pupils. Put in another way,
the teacher is not (or should not be) merely a communi-
cator of knowledge, unconcerned with the means whereby
this knowledge is acquired and the uses to which it is put.
The teacher is a kind of psychological diagnostician and
tactician vitally concerned with how children acquire and
utilize knowledge and skill. That a child has obtained the
highest scores on achievement tests should not be cause for
satisfaction in the teacher unless she has concluded that
these scores reflect a way of, and attitudes towards, learning
conducive toward productive and independent problem-
solving in the future. The means of learning affect the ends
of learning.

In the present chapter, we shall describe some pilot attempts on our part to approach the problems of teacher
training in a new kind of way. We do not dignify what we
have done over a three-year period by calling it "a study,"
because we did not proceed in a manner which would allow
either for the evaluation of hypotheses or comparison with
other procedures. We proceeded as we did in the hope that
after a period of time we could form some opinion about
the practicality of what we intended to do and, as important, feel more secure in the knowledge that we were asking
the right questions. In any event, we have set down here a
description of what we did, why we did it, and the reactions
of those (instructors and students) who participated. We
are aware that these reactions are biased, that is, they are
not independent and objective measures of the effects of
what we did.

The Setting

Our pilot attempts at a different way of training teachers took place at a multipurpose college which previously had been a teachers' college. The major focus of this college was still almost exclusively the training of teachers for elementary-school work. Our attempts took place in the Special Education department, which had as its main emphasis the preparation of teachers for work with the heterogeneous groups of children ordinarily found in special classes.[1] The Special Education department was located in a new building containing a classroom with an adjoining observation room capable of comfortably seating fifteen to eighteen students. The two rooms were separated by large one-way mirrors and, in addition, there was an audio system which allowed the observers to hear all that was going on in the classroom. The entrance to the observation room was through a seminar room.

The Pilot Year

In this pilot year, the special class to be observed was transported one morning a week from a local public school. The number in the class varied from twelve to fifteen children ranging in age from eight to fourteen. The student

[1] The composition of a class of retarded children is usually quite variable, ranging from those who are indisputably subnormal to those who are at least of borderline intellectual status, from those with some, to those with no physical or neurological handicaps, and from those who present no behavior problem to those who are difficult-management problems. For our purposes, it made little or no difference whether this was a special or regular class. Our focus with the college students in the observation seminar to be described was on processes and problems of observation. After three years of conducting such a seminar, no one (students, faculty, visitors) raised the problem of whether the classroom we were observing was appropriate to a seminar for college students, regardless of whether they were going to be special- or regular-class teachers.

observers were all beginning their junior year. They had not had any education courses and had spent practically no time at all in an elementary school classroom. There were fifteen college students in this seminar, all of whom had volunteered to participate. There was no course credit, and the time they gave was over and beyond the time required for carrying a normal course load.

At the first meeting of the seminar the following was said:

As you know, each time we will be meeting, the classroom beyond the observation room will contain a special class from one of our local schools. We will usually begin each meeting by observing the class for fifteen to twenty minutes after which we will come back to this seminar room (which adjoins the observation room) and take up whatever questions occurred to you during the observations. It is impossible to observe a class or any social gathering for this length of time without questions popping into your mind or without coming to some sort of conclusion or opinion. The one obligation which you have is to bring into the open your reactions to any observation. To the extent that you can feel free to articulate your reactions, you and the rest of us will learn from each other. One of the things you must guard against is keeping your ideas, questions, and opinions to yourself because you do not know whether they are right or wrong. If you do remain silent you, of course, increase the chances that you will be unable to evaluate your reactions other than in a subjective, private manner. This is an opportunity to learn, by which we mean an opportunity to change your ways of thinking and acting. If you do not actively participate in this market place of ideas, you will be shortchanging yourself. At this moment, you probably look upon your two instructors (Blatt and Sarason) as "experts" with whom it would be foolhardy for you to disagree. We do not view ourselves in this way, and we hope that it will not be too long before you see that we do not observe everything, and that we will be disagreeing with each other. Because we have had more experience than you should not intimidate you into automatically mistrusting or devaluating your reactions.

Our discussions following the initial observation will vary in duration, but we will always be going back to the observation room at least one more time during the course of the morning. Now let us go and observe.

There were three reasons for these introductory remarks. First, previous studies (Davidson, Sarason, 1961), as well as countless informal observations, had indicated to us how widely teachers differed in the scope of what they observed as well as in the validity of their observations. It is the rare teacher who is aware that observations are always selective in nature (one cannot observe everything) and that one of the most potent sources of selection is one's own personal values. We could say that most teachers are unaware of the degree to which the content of what they say they see, as well as the variety of things they observe, are functions of subjective factors which, in the light of their unawareness, they cannot begin to control. It would be surprising if the situation were otherwise, inasmuch as teachers receive little or no training, either in the nature and problems of observation, or in how observation affects what one does. For example, teachers frequently fail to distinguish between an observation of overt behavior and an inference about covert behavior. It is one thing to observe that a child has failed a certain task, and it is quite another thing to make inferences about why he failed. Such a distinction would be of no practical significance if the observer were not required to react to the child. But a teacher does react, and if she is not aware that her reaction will, in part, be based on inferences about covert behavior, and that the process of inference is sufficiently tricky so as to force one to reflect before taking action, the teacher's reaction to the child may at best be ineffective and at worst harmful.

A second reason for these introductory remarks stems from the fact that these students had rarely, if ever, been put into a situation where they were on their own, that is, where they had to decide what they would observe, evaluate, and articulate. In other words, they were not told what to look for, and whatever conclusions they came to had to be justified in ways other than by instructor-fed information. By structuring the situation in this way, we hoped to be able to illustrate for these students the differences between the passive approach to problem solving and one in which one's own capacities and initiative were important ingredients. Ultimately, of course, we hoped that awareness of this problem in their own learning would influence the ways in which they would structure the learning situation for their future pupils, an influence which would be facilitated in the course of observations of the children in the adjoining classroom.

A third reason for structuring the seminar as we did has to do with the self-attitudes of teachers, more specifically, the marked tendency among teachers to view themselves in their professional role in a derogatory manner. There are many reasons for such devaluation, but one of the most important is based on the implicit assumption that the teacher should be adequate, or equally effective, with all children and all problems in her class. In our opinion, this is as presumptuous an expectation as one could make and, in our experience, is not made for any other profession. It is difficult, and frequently impossible, for a teacher to say—to other teachers, administrators, and lay people—that there are children and problems to which she feels inadequate and ineffective. Aside from contributing to an unhealthy professional attitude, this situation frequently inhibits the teacher from seeking the kind of consultative help she needs. By structuring the seminar as we did, we hoped to bring this assumption out into the open so that these students might see how being able to say "I don't know," or recognizing that there are limits to their effectiveness, is an important factor in the learning (changing) process not only for themselves but for the children in their care.

The Behavior of the Students

What were the ways in which the students responded to the observation periods in the first few meetings? We were not surprised to find that one of the major obstacles to discussion was what appeared to be a fear of expressing an opinion which might be regarded as wrong. It seemed as if they had been sitting in the observation room preoccupied with questions such as "What am I supposed to look for?", "Who am *I* to pass judgment on this teacher?", etc. Because the two instructors did not offer ideas or starting points for discussion, the first few sessions contained a number of thundering silences. Although we anticipated such difficulties, we confess that we were taken aback at the degree to which these students were unable to verbalize their reactions, that is, to observe and react in a spontaneous kind of way unfettered by what they were supposed to observe and how they were to react.

On several occasions in the first two meetings, a couple of students explicitly verbalized that they were not sure how they were supposed to observe. To such statements, the response was essentially a condensation of the introductory remarks emphasizing that it was difficult, if not impossible, to observe any social group without questions coming to mind.

As might be expected in a group of fifteen students, there are usually two or three students who have no hesitation in expressing opinions, particularly when they are asked to present them, and it was these students who undoubtedly gave courage to the rest to begin to participate in discussion. From the third meeting on, the majority of the students showed little or no hesitancy in spontaneously presenting their reactions to the observations.

In earlier portions of this book, we indicated our agreement with the criticism that school children tend to be taught in a manner reflecting the unverbalized assumption that education consists of what you put into children. Teaching that has the elicitation and reinforcement of a child's curiosities, ideas, and special talents as its focus is all too rare; it enables a child to feel comfortable when thinking independently; it avoids his becoming a passive, uncritical recipient of knowledge. Our experience with the student group confirmed what we had long believed: The teacher's conception of how one educates children is a reflection of how she was educated and the role assigned to her as a learner. The struggle our students had in recognizing that their prepotent response was to seek direction from others is significant not only for the evaluation of their previous academic experiences, but for what it portends about the role they will adopt when they are teaching children. It is appropriate at this point to note that this prepotent way of responding was one of the most frequently discussed problems in the seminar. Instances were never wanting in the discussions to illustrate how this response-tendency affects observation, how it affects their conception of the learning process, how it tends to make for undue dependence on technique and formula, and how it underlies one's conception of oneself as a professional person. We should emphasize that the instances used to illustrate these problems were always derived from events which all of us observed: teacher-child interactions in the classroom, the kinds of questions directed at the two instructors, and the manner or style with which these questions were asked (undue deference, implicit self-derogation). Here, as in all else we attempted to do, discussion of principles and theory was based on events in which instructors and students were participants.

We will now list and briefly discuss other reactions of the students to the observations:

1. One of the reactions the students found both enlightening and disturbing concerned the range of individual differences among the children in the class. The following is a paraphrase of what a number of the students said (particularly in the earlier phases of our seminar): "I always knew that no two people were alike but I never really appreciated what this meant for a teacher. Each of these children is as different from each other as day from night. In our psychology courses we were told that you cannot teach

each child in the same way, and that certainly hits you in the face when you are observing this class, but we never really understood what this meant for teaching." What was disturbing to the students was how one teacher could become aware of and handle, academically and interpersonally, such a range of individual differences.

It should be noted that the teacher of the class being observed was, in our opinion, an unusually competent one. She was an ebullient, warm, self-confident individual who was a "natural" combination of teacher and psychologist. As we shall see later, the degree of her competence presented problems to the future conduct of the project. In any event, the students explicitly verbalized their concern that they would not be able to handle a class as this teacher did. In fact, at least two of the students said that after watching this teacher they felt that they had not had a realistic conception of what was involved in teaching, and that perhaps they had made a mistake in deciding on a teaching career. These kinds of reactions allowed us to focus on two questions: How did this teacher adapt herself and her techniques to individual differences among the children? What were the assumptions or principles which seemed to underlie her behavior and techniques? Whenever these questions were raised, discussion was frequently halted so that we could all make further observations relevant to a particular aspect of the problem, for example, to observe a particular child or an aspect of the teacher's behavior. In addition, the discussion was sometimes halted so that the teacher could join us in order to answer questions (usually pertaining to *why* she did something) which had been raised by the students or instructors.

2. The second reaction was less a reaction of the students than a consequence (introduced by the instructors) of what was happening at a certain point of time in our meetings. Observing a classroom of children is, in principle, similar to observing or perceiving any external event involving animate or inanimate objects. We refer here to the fact that

certain features of what we are observing stand out, while
others are a kind of background. In the case of observing
a classroom of children, we can predict that certain children, far more than others, will be in the center of one's
observations. The behavior-problem child, the obviously
bright child, a particularly pretty or ugly child—these are
the types of children who, so to speak, catch our eyes. In
the classroom we were observing, there was a handful of
children who excited the interest of a majority of the students and occupied a significant portion of discussion time.
These were fruitful discussions involving the problems of
how to arouse, maintain, and change motivation, and the
role of materials as aids in the learning process, the limitations of such aids, and the importance of manner of presentation of problems to children. Discussion of these problems
always stemmed from and involved children and events
which all of us had observed. As a result of these discussions, the teacher occasionally was requested to structure
the class the following week around a particular problem
(reading, arithmetic, letter writing, etc.) , so as to allow us
to check on points raised in the discussion.

After several meetings in which this handful of children
had occupied a significant amount of discussion time, the
students were asked why they were concentrating on these
few children. Were these children intrinsically more interesting than the others? Were the problems being discussed
not characteristic of the other children? Did these other
children not present teaching and handling problems? In
so confronting the class the instructors hoped to illustrate
several points. First, how selective the process of observing
could be; second, how easy it can be for a teacher to focus
her attention and energies on a few children to the neglect
of others; third, how important it is for a teacher to learn
to ask, "Whom am I *not* thinking about?" or "Who isn't
causing me to think about him?" In other words, one of
the major obstacles to a teacher's taking the nature of individual differences among her children seriously is the

failure to have learned to reflect about how her attention, observations, and behavior are determined by the particular composition of her class. This confrontation had an immediate effect upon the students, not only in the sense of an insight about what they had been doing, but in an eagerness to return to the observation room in order to focus on children who had barely, or had not at all, been entering our discussions.

3. After nine weeks (one morning a week) of meetings, the students were required to practice teach for nine weeks in a regular class in an elementary school. The two instructors had nothing to do with the practice teaching either in terms of when it was taking place, its duration, or its supervision. Following the practice-teaching period, the students returned to the seminar. The majority of these students returned set to ask one question: Why, in nine weeks of observing the class in the adjoining room had we *never* witnessed a single instance of a discipline problem? The children were relaxed and happy, were motivated to learn, and obviously enjoyed their school experience. Having asked this question, the students went on to describe how quickly in their practice-teaching experience, usually on day one, they encountered and felt inadequate about disciplinary problems. How did this teacher manage to have no disciplinary problems, particularly in the light of the school history of the children in the class? Before the practice-teaching period, the instructors had been quite aware of the absence of disciplinary problems but had refrained from bringing the matter up until it had come into the awareness of the students.

The instructors did not attempt to answer the question but, rather, initiated a discussion about the complexities and trickiness of the observation process. Following this, the students were asked to begin a series of observations with the aim of attempting to answer for themselves the question they had raised. It was pointed out to the students that it was easy for the instructors to give an "answer" to their question, but that this was not necessarily the best way to handle their curiosity. They, just as in the case of the children they would be teaching, needed to strive to formulate an answer to a problem they encountered. *It is important to emphasize that throughout the seminar the identity between how teachers are or should be taught and how their pupils are or should be taught was discussed wherever appropriate to the experience of the students.*

The answers which the students formulated to their question were cogent, although incomplete in varying degrees. The fact that this teacher was warm to her pupils was a glimpse of the obvious. The students went on to point out that this teacher had explicit rules governing her own as well as her pupils' behavior, and that she adhered to these rules fairly; she made it explicit that they were to try to do as much for themselves as possible, and that she was available to them whenever they needed her help; it was made easy for these children to verbalize their difficulties, and it was the responsibility of the other members of the class to try to understand the difficulties of others and to try to help. One student summed up much of what the students were saying in this way: "You get a lot of talk about how you have to respect your pupils and that there is something about each of them that you can develop. When you watch Miss ——— you *know* she respects each one. It's as if she really respects each one and is going to bring out the best in them."

It seems appropriate at this point to describe an observation made during the time that we were discussing this unusual teacher. The appropriateness of the observation resides not only in what it reflects about the teacher (and what it demonstrated to the students), but also in that it indicates the potentialities of our approach to teacher training.

When we entered the observation room, one of the children, Amy, was obviously the center of the other children's attention. We soon learned that the evening before Amy had been on a children's TV program and had been asked questions by Happy the Clown. Everyone had known that Amy was to be on the program and, needless to say, most had seen the program. After the children had been talking among each other for some time, the teacher casually said, "You know, Amy, some of the children did not see the program. Why not tell them the kind of questions Happy asked you?" Amy, the least of whose problems was talking, proceeded on at some length never, however, indicating what questions had been put to her. The teacher waited for an opportune time and then said:

Teacher: Wasn't the first question he asked you what your name was?
Amy: That's right. I told him my name was Amy ———
Teacher: Then he asked you what school you went to?
Amy: Yes. I told him I went to ——— School.
Teacher: Didn't he then ask you who your teacher was?
Amy: Yes. I told him it was Miss ———.
Teacher: Then he asked you what grade you were in?

To this question Amy could only stare at the teacher with a helpless, distressed look on her face and was obviously at a loss for words. What then came out was that Amy had answered Happy's question by saying she was in the fourth grade whereas in fact she was (and knew she was) in a *special class*. The teacher expressed surprise at Amy's answer and wondered if Amy were ashamed of being in a special class. Did the others feel the same way, she asked? There then followed a thirty minute discussion in which all the children verbalized what it meant to be in a special class, how it affected their relationships with friends and other children in the school, and how, in fact, most of them felt ashamed of being considered stupid.

All of us in the observation room were aware that we had observed what it means to be able to sense and identify with how a child feels, the significance of self-attitudes for the learning process, and the casual, but expert manner in which self-attitudes had been brought into the open, not because "openness" was a virtue in itself, but because of its significance for motivation and learning. We might note that this teacher closed the discussion with a "lecture" on the nature of individual differences which left little to be desired.

4. The last major reaction which we present involved the student's practice-teaching experience and a comparison

between it and the observation seminar. It is hard to convey the strength and diversity of criticism which the students leveled against the manner in which the practice teaching was handled. These criticisms are briefly listed below:

1. Too much of the student's time was spent in assigned "busywork," record keeping, and test scoring.

2. A great deal of the student's time (usually evenings) was spent in preparation of lesson plans which the student only infrequently had an opportunity to try out.

3. The relationship between the student and the master teacher was not one which enabled the student to ask questions, discuss issues, or verbalize disagreements.

4. Supervision, in the sense that the student's actual teaching behavior and handling of pupils was searchingly reviewed in terms of psychological principles, the degree to which individual differences were taken account of, and the nature of the learning process, was rare. It was as if the student teacher were viewed as a kind of mechanic who had to be taught the technical know-how.

When the students talked about their practice-teaching experiences, we did not ask them to compare their experiences to what we had been doing in the observation seminar, although obviously they may have thought that we were interested in such a comparison.[2] In any event, many of their criticisms of the practice-teaching experiences were based on comparisons with the observation seminar. This was particularly the case when they discussed their relationship to the master teacher, that is, the lack of opportunity

[2] It was our hope, of course, that what took place in the observation seminar would affect the student's perception of his practice-teaching experience, although the seminar was never discussed as a preparation for practice teaching. That the comparison which the students were making between the practice-teaching and seminar experiences reflected their own thinking, rather than a desire to tell us what we may have wanted to hear, is indicated by their impatience upon returning in initiating the discussion about behavior problems.

to raise questions, voice disagreements, and to utilize their own ideas on how to conduct themselves with the pupils. Another issue around which they made comparisons was the failure of the master teacher to discuss the individual differences among the children and how these differences affected pedagogical technique.

It would be unfair if we left the reader with the impression that the practice-teaching experience of these students was of little value. The students explicitly pointed out that spending nine weeks in a classroom and actually having the responsibility of teaching and handling children was valuable to them. Essentially, their criticism reflected an awareness of how much more valuable the experience could have been.

The Second and Third Years

In the previous pages of this chapter, we endeavored to convey a picture of what went on in the seminar. In planning for subsequent years, several factors had to be taken into account. The first of these was the choice of teacher for the class being observed. Was the first-year teacher too good for demonstration purposes? Would it have been more helpful to the students if they had been able to observe a teacher who made more "mistakes," who was less able to adapt herself and her techniques to the individual needs of the children, and who was a less sensitive observer? Ideally, of course, it would have been best if we could have observed several teachers over the period of the year, but this was beyond our means. We never had to make a decision about the first-year teacher because of a second factor affecting our planning. This second factor stemmed from our awareness and the students' criticism of the limitations of a one-morning-a-week seminar. The students felt that they would have gained more from the seminar if it had been held more frequently, if they could have actually taught the children, if they could have had more opportunities to observe them, and if certain aspects of teaching (reading, for example) could have been explored more thoroughly. These considerations required that we have the class in session at least each morning. Because it could not be arranged for the first-year teacher and her class to spend each morning at the college, another teacher and her class were utilized in the subsequent years.

Our experiences in the subsequent years were essentially similar to what we have already described. As we expected, the change in teachers certainly affected the nature of the discussions. It had been our intention, after the first year, to accede to the request of the students that the seminar continue through their senior year. However, this turned out to be impossible because of the large number of juniors-to-be who signed up for the seminar.

At the beginning of this chapter, we indicated that we were going to attempt to describe a new approach to teacher training. In Chapter 2, we described the conventional ways in which teachers are trained; it seems appropriate at this point to distinguish between those approaches and ours.

The most obvious difference between our approach and those currently employed resides in differing conceptions of supervision. As was indicated in the previous chapter, supervision of the student, be it in a so-called laboratory course, teacher-training period, field trip, etc., is usually extremely brief. Fairly frequently it is nonexistent. In the approach we have described, it is clear that a large amount of supervision time is given students. In fact, in our observation, seminar instructors *always* were with or available to the students. We realize fully that a lot of supervision time need not in itself be a virtue, and in describing our experiences we emphasize not the amount of time, but what we consider to be a way of structuring the relationship between students and instructors, which is different from more conventional procedures. Briefly, and to recapitulate: The students were rarely *given* ideas or starting points; they had to subject their ideas, opinions, and suggestions to discussion; they were more or less forced to learn to give expression to and to depend upon *their* curiosity; they could express their puzzlements and ignorance without viewing them as signs of stupidity but as aids to productive learning; and they were enabled to see for themselves the complexity and selectivity of their own observational processes and their effects on action. To accomplish these things, it is far from sufficient to say to students: "Be curious. Use your own ideas. Do not be afraid to be wrong," etc. Unless students actually begin to respond in these ways and in so doing experience an awareness of a change in their thinking and perspective, verbal suggestions are not likely to be effective. *It is essential to our approach to expect that students will and must struggle, because learning to think independently and to utilize one's own intellectual resources is never easy, particularly when previous learning has been of the passive, dependent variety.*

Another difference between what we attempted to do and the more traditional approaches to teacher training did, initially at least, require the presentation of an idea to the students. We hope that in our description of what we did, we conveyed to the reader that many of our discussions involved an awareness and discussion of how we (instructors and students) were learning. Once the students spontaneously began to utilize the seminar in the manner we had hoped, and the nature of the learning process in the seminar was under discussion, we asked the students to think about and compare the ways in which children are ordinarily taught and the way in which they, the students, were learning. Could it not be that many of the things the students vociferously criticized about their own college training also characterized the ways in which teachers taught children? Did teachers tend to spoon-feed children, avoid coming to grips with their curiosity, inhibit disagreements and nonconformity, and reward intellectual passivity? It was these kinds of questions which enabled the students to see that the principles of and conditions for productive learning held for the training of the teacher as well as the children she would be teaching.

What was obviously crucial to our approach was the opportunity for instructors and students together to observe a teacher and her class over a long period of time. One of the most important aspects of such an opportunity is the basis provided for the predictions made on the basis of observations. It is our impression that the observations of the students, which they would bring up for discussion, frequently involved three types of considerations: a description of the overt event, inferences about the internal or covert states of the children or teacher, and an implicit prediction about the consequences of whatever they observed. For example, the students would frequently present their observations and, explicitly or implicitly, these observations would contain judgments about the consequences of the event for the future progress of the child. Fairly frequently, the students would describe a child, unaware that the description implied either a particular future status or a certain level of intellectual potential as distinguished from performance. One of the major functions of the instructors was to make explicit the implied predictions so that they could be evaluated by the students through further observation over varying lengths of time. It was always a highlight (to the instructors, at least) of a meeting when a student came out of the observation room eager to describe something which was at variance with an earlier prediction. In the course of discussion of these and other problems, one principle was always emphasized: First, once we have pinned a label on a child, our observations of him tend to pay more attention to what fits in with that label than what is discrepant with it. Consequently, we tend to "prove" our initial prediction when, in fact, contrary evidence has simply been overlooked.

Another advantage of long-term observation is that we

can count on being able to observe and discuss almost every kind of important problem a teacher encounters.[3] In short, we deal not with an ideal situation, but with a representative one.

There is another aspect of our approach to which we have made only passing reference. We refer here to the role of didactic lectures in the observation seminar. It will be recalled that the students were all college juniors who, in their first two college years, had taken liberal arts courses. They all had taken some psychology courses, and at the same time that they were participating in the observation seminar they were taking courses in methods, curriculum materials, etc. However, in conducting the seminar, the instructors were in no way influenced by the fact that the students were taking or had taken certain courses. We are certainly not advocates of the position that lectures are ineffective or useless, and nothing that we have said should be construed as recommending the abolition of lecture courses, although we clearly advocate that, in the case of teacher training at least, their limitations should be recognized and their appropriate integration with an approach like or akin to ours undertaken. For example, we did, from time to time, give formal lectures in the seminar, but this was done only when it became apparent that the students had come upon a problem about which they needed knowledge, or about which they were misinformed, or about which there had been some misunderstanding when it was discussed in other settings.

One such problem which came up often concerned the use of psychological test data by teachers. It was apparent that these students had a strange combination of attitudes towards psychological tests. They had little or no grasp of psychological principles underlying the development and use of tests, they unduly and uncritically accepted and respected test scores, and at the same time there was

[3] As we indicated earlier, this was not true with the first class and teacher we utilized. In the subsequent year, however, the students did observe every major problem a teacher can encounter.

a strong tendency to derogate the idea that psychological test scores were very meaningful. Psychological-test reports were available on each child in the classroom. It was in the course of discussing these reports together with the observations of the children that these attitudes were most clearly expressed. Consequently, several lectures were given on psychological tests, with the focus on their uses and limitations.

We make no strong claim that these lectures were very effective or clarifying. We are here merely trying to illustrate under what conditions lectures may be most effective, that is, when the students, as a result of their observations, have come upon a problem or present it in a way which clearly reveals an ignorance or misapprehension of information and concepts. We might say here, on the basis of long experience with a wide variety of teachers in different settings, that as a group, teachers have no foundation for understanding and utilizing the psychological test data ordinarily provided to them. This in itself would not be very serious were it not for the fact that too frequently teachers' behavior and attitudes toward children are influenced either by giving undue weight to test scores, by unjustifiably disregarding them, or by serious misinterpretation of their meaning. We could, in a book much larger than the present one, give instance after instance in which a teacher misinterpreted the meaning of psychological test data. A major part of the problem is that courses in educational testing apparently are taught in a way which used to be characteristic of mathematics courses, that is, with a dependence on the rote learning of formuli and computational steps and "text book" examples, which extinguish interest and reinforce anxiety and self-derogation. The discrepancy between the kinds of problems utilized in such courses and the kinds of problems teachers are faced with is, to be charitable, marked.

The experiences we have described in this chapter raise a number of questions about the applicability of our approach to other aspects of teacher training. How applicable is it to the practice-teaching periods? Into what kinds of courses can such an approach be integrated? What kinds of personnel can supervise such experiences? How early in the college curriculum should such an approach be available to students? These questions, as well as other problems in teacher training, will be taken up in the next chapter. It is appropriate at this time to remind the reader that we did not describe our approach in this chapter in order to prove that what we did is superior to what others do. Obviously, we believe that what we have described is superior to conventional procedures. Whether, in fact, this is so will have to be determined by future research.

5

Implications and
Recommendations

In the first chapter of this book we described the teacher
as a kind of psychological diagnostician and tactician, a
characterization meant to convey the opinion that the
teacher, far from being a mere transmitter of knowledge, is
one who elicits and reinforces the child's intellectual curiosity and strivings so that the acquisition of knowledge is a
productive affair, that is, whatever knowledge and skills are
acquired increase the child's capacity independently to discover and cope with new problems. To accomplish such a
goal requires, among other things, that the teacher have not
only a thorough grasp of psychological principles of child
development, but the ability to observe the different ways
in which these principles are manifested in different children and how recognition of such differences affects a
teacher's tactics. It was this kind of view of the nature of
teaching which gave rise to the studies briefly described on
page 59 and to the development of the observation seminar described in the last chapter.

One question which arises about the role of the observation seminar in teacher training concerns when the students should participate in it. As was made clear in Chapter 2, there is, at present, fair agreement that the purely professional aspects of teacher training should be preceded by a firm grounding in the liberal arts and science areas. In the case of the traditional teachers' college, this has come to mean that the first two years of the program should be devoted primarily, if not exclusively, to nonprofessional education. In Master of Arts in Teaching programs (Keppel, 1961) all, or almost all, professional training takes place after the traditional undergraduate program has been completed. Inasmuch as we have expressed agreement with this trend, at the same time that we have indicated that it is far from a solution to more effective teaching, it may come as a surprise that we would recommend that something akin to the observation seminar should come as early as possible after the student has decided to go into teaching.[1] We make such a recommendation because we do not view such a seminar as a "how-to-do-it" or methods course. We view such a

[1] The problem of when such a seminar would be taken is not unrelated to the problem of who should be allowed to become a teacher. In our teachers' colleges, at least, the criteria for selection are minimal and irrelevant to the issue of who should be encouraged to become a teacher. A high school diploma and an average or above-average intelligence-test score are the most frequent criteria used in selection—objective criteria, to be sure, but at best amazingly incomplete and, at worst, irrelevant. In the Masters of Arts in Teaching programs, the situation is somewhat different and only somewhat more defensible: The students are older (they have had at least three years of college), they have higher intelligence test scores (by virtue of having successfully finished three years of college, and coming from colleges having much higher test score requirements for admission than is the case in teachers' colleges), and obviously they must have had more education than is represented by a high school diploma. It may also be that the students in the MAT programs have arrived in a more mature way at the decision to enter teaching, although there is no evidence on this point. The problem of selection is raised here, because it obviously makes a difference if an observation seminar contains students varying enormously in strength and sources of motivation for teaching, personality, intellectual level, and maturity.   '

seminar as an opportunity whereby the student can discover that the processes of observation and inference are not only complex, but also ways of investigation requiring sustained intellectual concentration and critical self-scrutiny. One might say that the goal is to have the student experience the difference between active and passive ways of observing and how this difference affects action.

We would expect that the length of time the student would spend in such a seminar, as well as the conduct and contents of the seminar, would vary depending on whether one is dealing with freshmen, sophomores, etc. However, the opportunity for the student to utilize, develop, and change his capacity for observation and self-scrutiny would always be in the focus. It has been pointed out (Griswold, 1959) that the term *liberal* arts reflects the concept that such studies are meant to have a liberating influence upon the students, that is, to liberate the students' capacities by developing new perspectives and habits of critical thinking. The achievement of such a liberating influence is or should be the primary goal of such an observation seminar. When viewed in this way, our recommendation about early exposure to such a seminar cannot be viewed as being contradictory to the position that the training of teachers in the liberal arts and sciences has not been sufficiently intensive or extensive.

A second question arising about the observation seminar concerns its relation to other courses in the preprofessional years. The courses most relevant to the purposes of the seminar are those in psychology, particularly in child psychology or development. At the present time, these courses are typically taught in lecture fashion, with all the limitations that almost exclusive dependence on the lecture method imposes. Over the years we have had any number of students say, "Yes, I had a course in child psychology and I think I learned a good deal in it. However, when I really began to work with children I realized how much I did not know." It is easy to interpret such a statement as reflecting the type of mind interested only in knowledge that can be used for practical purposes. Frequently, this interpretation is correct, but equally frequently it has reflected the awareness that it is one thing to be told and to read about facts and principles of child development and another thing to recognize them when having to handle children. One of the frequent criticisms of their psychology courses by the students in our observation seminars was the lack of opportunity to observe, in a live situation, how psychological principles, concepts, and generalizations could be derived. It should be made clear that this complaint was not made on the basis that what they learned in these courses was of no use in teaching. In fact, these complaints frequently arose before the student had any teaching experience. The complaint, probably because of what they were experiencing in the observation seminar, reflected an awareness of the difference between knowledge derived from passive attendance at lectures and that derived from observation of live illustrations.

We would not recommend that the kind of observation seminar described in the previous chapter be utilized in conjunction with the child psychology course. For one thing, the observation seminar has, as we have tried to emphasize, goals which, in fact, may be incompatible with those in a child psychology course. For example, in the seminar there was little or no attempt to transmit an organized body of knowledge, while for the purposes of a child psychology course, the observations might well have to be more structured for the students by the instructor. In addition, the goals of the observation seminar can be achieved by utilizing pretty much any one classroom, whereas the range of ages covered in a child psychology course precludes utilization of one group of children. There is more to child development than coverage of the school years, and there is more to the school years than what takes place in a classroom. To the extent that a child psychology course concentrates on the child-in-school, the intellectual perspective of the student is being unjustifiably narrowed by consideration of professional training.

What we do recommend for the child psychology course is a series of closely supervised observational experiences which has as its goal the exemplification of principles and concepts considered in the lecture situation. Aside from the degree of close supervision, these experiences resemble the observation seminar in two important respects. First, the student should be expected and encouraged to express disagreements and questions. Second, the experiences should be sufficiently sustained over time so that observation of change is a real possibility. In recommending these experiences as an integral part of the child psychology course (or the educational psychology or psychology of learning courses), we do not have in mind making such courses more "practical." What we do have in mind is to give the student the opportunity to see as well as hear the bases for what are considered important principles.[2]

A third question arising about the role of the observation seminar concerns its relation to the usual methods and curriculum materials courses (Chapter 2). It is these courses which have been among the main targets of the critics of teacher training, and rightly so. Aside from their time-consuming nature, these courses, which are admittedly "practical" in aim, are usually very impractical, in that students find them of no great help. (It should be said that if many of the critics of teacher training had been more familiar with the teachers' colleges, they would have discovered years

[2] One does not label an introductory chemistry or physics course as "practical" because it has laboratory periods in which principles and concepts discussed in class are illustrated in different ways either by the student or instructor. Similarly, one does not deride a math instructor who at every opportunity attempts to illustrate the significances of problems by relating them to experiences within the ken of students. The aim of such demonstrations is to aid the student in grasping principles. We conceive of the observation seminar and the series of experiences which should accompany psychology courses in the same light.

ago that the students there were among the most cogent critics of their own training.) There is little doubt that the major defects of the methods courses, in particular, are threefold. First, the emphasis is on how to teach certain subject matter (reading, arithmetic, etc.), but this rarely is accompanied by opportunities for the student to try out the methods. Second, where the student does have such opportunity, it is usually of short duration, and supervision is minimal or nonexistent. Third, and this is felt most keenly by students (see page 104), what the students obtain in these courses too often has little relevance for teaching a class of children who vary considerably (as is almost always the case) in their achievement in any particular subject matter or skill.

We think it appropriate at this point to present (without comment) an excerpt from a tape recording of a discussion we had with a group of college students who had already had one practice-teaching experience. This discussion was not part of the observational seminar previously described. The students were brought together and presented with this question: "You all have had nine weeks of practice teaching. What are the relationships between all you learned and experienced in college and what you experienced in practice teaching?"

(At this point in the discussion, "Student 1" has been explaining a problem he had with a particular child.)

Student 1: I didn't take her out of the room because of the training teacher. He didn't believe in it.

Instructor 1: Why?

Student 1: Because of what might happen in the hallway.

Instructor 1: I don't quite understand.

Student 1: The teacher described extreme examples of what might happen.

Student 2: When you take the child outside, it is the child's word against the teacher's and the child might exaggerate what happens.

Student 3: Once, I took a child outside the room, he apologized, and went back to his seat. The training teacher was in the room.

Student 4 and other students: We were told never to do this.

Student 1: I did this once when a child threatened me. The teacher told me never to do it again.

Instructor 1: I am very puzzled about this. It appears as if many teachers feel this way. It represents a degree of intimidation of the teacher which is very unhealthy. It doesn't speak well of the teacher's self-attitudes and self-respect.

Instructor 2: This characterizes many teachers. It isn't uncommon. During my first year of teaching one of the first things I was told by the principal was that if you keep a child in after school make sure the door is open. It is not unusual advice for student teachers to receive.

Instructor 1: This brings up a problem, the problem of how the role of the teacher in our society has changed in the past twenty, thirty, and forty years. What it suggests is that the teacher is intimidated in the sense of doing what he or she may think is the right thing to do. It results in a kind of conformity in which the teacher as a person and a professional loses out as well as the child. This is what is disturbing about it.

Student 1: Years ago if the teacher corrected a child and the child went home and told the parent, the parent was with the teacher almost 100%. It seems that now, it is just the opposite. If a child went home and told the parent that the teacher hit him with a ruler, the whole community would be down on the teacher.

Student 2: I would like to go back to the question of how college helped. I think that the content subjects have helped, but some of the theory courses stress the ideal situation too much. I taught at ——— School and that is as far from the ideal situation as you can get.

Instructor 2: What professional theory courses have you taken?

Student 2: Reading and language arts.

Instructor 2: Did you take those before student teaching?

Student 2: No, after.

Instructor 2: Then they had no effect on your student teaching?

Student 2: Right. The two courses stressed what you should do in this ideal situation with an ideal number of students. For example, an assignment was to draw up the ideal classroom situation. They figure all the students in the class would have about equal intelligence, they would all have the same initiative, come from a good family, whereas you don't usually get that in a school; you get a high reader and the low reader. If they based it more or less on the practicality of it, it would serve a purpose. But you go into a class and sit there for two hours and hear what you should or shouldn't do in the ideal situation and that is a waste of time.

Student 3: That's why I'm glad I went out teaching first, because if I had heard all this "ideal" and what you should do in the ideal situation, I would have been more lost than I was.

Instructor 2: In other words, you think that by not taking these methods courses before student teaching you were better off.

Student 3: Yes, the ones that I had, anyway.

Student 5: I don't think that the only problem is in the content of the methods taught, these ideal situations; I think that the major problem is the teachers that are teaching us. The way they treat us and . . .

Instructor 2: What courses are these?

Student 4: Reading and language arts. I don't think they bring out the important points. They just bring out the ideal situation and they take too much time on busy work as far as I am concerned.

Instructor 2: You said the way they teach you is a problem too. Tell us about it.

Student 4: They treat you like children rather than college students. For example, "Sit up straight, put your feet flat on the floor." We were talking among ourselves one day and we agreed that you could take the reading and language arts courses and make them one two-week course (other students agreed when this was said).

Instructor 1: I have heard this before.

Student 1: Why do they stress choral speaking for three or four weeks and then offer remedial reading for less than one period?

Student 2: We have choral speaking again in "Children's Literature," about two chapters in our book.

Student 3: It seems ridiculous to sit there for two hours and recite poems to each other.

Student 6: And practice your handwriting for an hour, I know that this is important, but . . .

Instructor 1: What is the student's image of himself as a professional person? In other words, in a sense you are saying that you have as little respect for some of the professional aspects of teacher training as some of the most vociferous critics have. In essence, you are agreeing with these critics who say that a lot of these courses concern busy work, as you put it, and I think it is well put.

Student 4: I don't think it is the material so much that we object to but the way in which it is given to us.

Student 2: If they had more of a clinical type work, if they had a method you could actually see, a method where one teacher taught different groups and subdivided the class into groups, it would be beneficial. My wife is a teacher and taught for about six years and she will say the same thing, that some of the theory courses could actually be thrown out because they are not practical.

Student 3: I think that if you take an honest opinion from each of us, and I am pretty sure we all passed the professional courses, we can say that we all passed without learning anything really new and without studying very much.

Instructor 2: In other words, you went through a semester without learning anything new of importance to you, and yet you passed the courses.

Student 7: Really, that's the way we feel. I do not think any of us did half the work we should have. We did not read the book. The tests were so ridiculous and simple that I think anybody with common sense could have passed them.

In initiating the observation seminar with college juniors, we were interested in seeing to what extent questions about teaching methods would spontaneously arise. From one standpoint, we hoped that a number of these questions would arise, because we assumed that this kind of seminar lent itself to observing and learning about teaching methods in a setting obviously similar to that in which the student would ultimately find himself. However, we feared that if too many of these questions arose, they could well defeat the purposes of the seminar as described in the previout chapter. Fortunately, questions and discussions about teaching methods arose to a noninterfering degree and were of such a content as to reinforce our opinion that such a seminar could well be adapted to the illustration, discussion, and trying out of methods for the teaching of arithmetic, reading, etc. In fact, the students themselves made the suggestion that there be a second meeting of the seminar (it met once a week) devoted exclusively to problems of teaching methods. What was heartening to us was the students' awareness that the purposes of the observation seminar were not identical with their need for exposure to and learning of teaching methods.

It is perhaps necessary at this point to elaborate on and clarify our recommendations about the role of the observation seminar. The seminar, as we have described it in the previous and early parts of the present chapter, would be a required experience for students as soon as they have decided on a teaching career.[3] In these early college years, the focus of the seminar would not be professional in nature, but rather an understanding of the complexity of the observational process and an inculcation of an attitude of critical inquiry toward self, others, and problems. A second recommendation was that the psychology courses (child, learning, etc.), which the students take in their preprofessional years, should have, as an integral part, some kind of observational seminar in which the student, under the type of supervision we have previously described, can observe, question, and discuss principles and problems raised in lectures and textbooks. We refrain from saying that this kind of seminar should be very similar to our observational seminar, because the purposes of the two may require different seminar structure and procedure. What would concern us, however, would be the tendency to ignore, or fail to see, what is the major principle guiding us: The student must, to whatever extent possible, be encouraged to learn independently and in a way which not only reinforces critical thinking, but increases the strength and range of his intellectual curiosity. We have seen too many field trips and classroom demonstrations to underestimate the tendency to spoon-feed students, effectively inhibit expression of their doubts and questions, and, in general, treat them as partic-

---

[3] We have chosen to talk about the role of the observation seminar in terms of the college years. In so doing, however, we would not want it overlooked that such a seminar can be an excellent basis for in-service training of those who are already teachers. As we indicated in the preface of this book, teachers, as a group are acutely aware of the inadequacy of their training for the complex task of guiding and stimulating children's learning. Such awareness is complicated by the knowledge that there is little they can do to remedy the situation. They could take more courses, but they take a dim view of what they could thereby gain. In our opinion, the observation seminar could be of considerable value to many teachers—at the least, it would be of more value than many of the graduate courses they take in order to obtain a master's degree for the purpose of receiving a salary increase.

ipants in some kind of advanced obedience course. A third recommendation involved an observation seminar by means of which much that is currently ineffectively taken up in the conventional methods courses would be more meaningfully experienced by the students.

We can no longer postpone discussion of what perhaps is the most serious obstacle to the initiation and successful execution of the observation seminar. We refer here to the type of personnel needed to conduct such a seminar. It is not difficult to state the qualifications which are necessary for conducting such a seminar. Clearly, such a person should have an understanding of and experience with a wide variety of children—their development, problems, and management. In addition, he should have a knowledge and understanding of the social psychology of a school, the functions and problems of teachers and teaching, and an awareness of the problems of translating psychological knowledge into plans of action practical within the classroom setting. Finally, and as important as any of the preceding, such a person must be able to act consistently with the belief that one of his major functions is to enable the students in the seminar to discover and experience for themselves (or with minimal guidance) the nature and dynamics of the observational process and its relation to learning. This requires not only a particular knowledge and orientation of certain aspects of perception and learning, but the ability to structure the seminar consistent with such knowledge and orientation.

There are several fields which train persons having the preceding qualifications in varying degrees. Clinical psychology, child psychology, psychiatry, and certain areas of social psychology are fields to which one would look for the kind of personnel needed for conducting an observation seminar. It is not necessary to detail the different ways in which these different fields tend to train persons lacking one or another of the qualifications described (in general terms) above. The most serious lack which they all share is that they train people who have little or no knowledge of what goes on in a school or classroom. One reason for this is that these people, in their training, simply have no meaningful contact with the school setting. Psychologists are trained in one part of the university, psychiatrists in another, while the teacher or educator, assuming the university has a department or school of education, is trained in still another part. The physical separation of these fields from each other would not be serious if it did not also reflect an attitude of derogation, on the part of the psychological disciplines, toward those in departments or schools of education—an attitude which historically allowed and forced the educationist to go it alone. However, we are not concerned here with history but in the description of those reality factors which are effective obstacles to the improvement of teacher training.

There are indications that graduate departments of psychology are becoming aware of the adverse implications of their estrangements from education. The concern of such departments derives from their recognition that they have little or nothing to do with the teaching of psychology in teachers' colleges, a setting in which a large percentage of all psychology courses in this country are taught. The teachers of psychology in this setting infrequently are those who have been fully trained in approved graduate departments of psychology. It would be disappointing indeed, if psychology's renewed interest in education did not go beyond "who teaches what" to a recognition of the classroom teacher as a variety of psychological observer, diagnostician, and tactician. Such a recognition cannot but lead both to more focused inquiries into what teachers do or expect to do and to a reformulation of the nature and goals of training (to which this book represents a small contribution).

There were two reasons for the preceding questioning of the qualifications of those who might conduct an observational seminar. One reason of course, was to make the point that the training and availability of such people were by no means unimportant considerations. A second reason was that raising such a question might set the stage more clearly for discussion of a crucial problem: How are master or critic teachers chosen, and what is or should be their function in supervising the student teacher? Earlier in this chapter (page 102), we presented excerpts from taped discussions with students after they had their first nine weeks of practice teaching. The beginning section of that excerpt was relevant to our present discussion. Below we present an excerpt with another group of students in the subsequent year. The procedure was somewhat different in that the group was asked to discuss the question ("What are the relationships between all you learned and experienced in college and what you experienced in practice teaching?") among themselves without the presence of the instructors who, after a half hour, returned to the room.

> Student 1: The second point we discussed was in relation to our training teachers and training periods. We came to the conclusion that if our training teachers would sit down with us and come right out and tell us that this is the objective for this, and this is what to look for, watch this reaction, etc., we would find it much more helpful. We also found that when we were supposed to be observing, they had us doing jobs around the room, watering plants, cutting paper, distracting us completely from what we were supposed to be doing.
>
> Instructor 1: Is this a general opinion?
>
> Students: (Some said yes, others said no.)
>
> Student 2: No. I had a student-teaching situation where I was told objectives and the teacher explained the curriculum to me. When I observed her teaching, I knew what she was going to do, why she was going to do it, and what she was going to do next.
>
> Student 1: That was a unique experience.
>
> Student 2: For that reason I probably started teaching

earlier than most of the student teachers. (Most students did very little teaching until the end of the practice teaching period.)

Student 3: My teacher would say, "Watch for these points," and then she would say, "Put up this bulletin board." You just never did have time to watch her if you did your other jobs.

Student 2: During my observation period I did nothing but observe. I did take a "story time" which was teaching, but I didn't do any bulletin board work or paper cutting, or anything like that.

Student 4: When we finally started to make out plans, we were told we had to put down "objectives" and "motivation." My teacher never even told me any of her objectives all the time I was there. I just had to watch and try to figure them out myself; in the beginning I had no idea.

Student 1: We felt that it would have been beneficial if something to this effect were injected into "sophomore orientation." Most of us walked into student teaching cold; we didn't realize anything. I don't know how the rest of them feel, but I had to feel my way through the whole thing. My teacher never told me anything. I read books, but I didn't find them helpful. I guess experience is the best teacher, but I think I did waste quite a bit of time just trying to figure out these different things.

Instructor 1: Did any of you feel that you should have had your curriculum materials courses before you went out student teaching?

Student 3: This point was discussed, but we were not in complete agreement on it. I felt that perhaps we should have been given about a week prior to going out, to get a review of what was expected of us and what we were to expect. If we had even this short time for preparation, it would have helped tremendously.

Student 1: Just a briefing would have helped us.

Instructor 1: How did your seminars with your campus teacher help you in overcoming hurdles in the classroom?

Student 1: How can he help us? He can't give us something we can go back and do, because they are two different situations. We are taking our school problems to the college professor, and he is in a situation where he can't tell us what to do in our school.

Instructor 2: What is the function of this seminar on campus during your practice teaching?

Student 1: I think to discuss what we have been experiencing in our classroom. We can tell him that we were short on preparation and that our master teachers weren't helping us very much. What he does about this we don't know.

Instructor 1: How often are you visited by the campus teacher?

Student 1: He occasionally walked in and out of the room. I think he stopped in my room twice.

Instructor 1: Is this in the nine-week period?

Student 1: In the beginning he came to see if I had lesson plans started and then he left. He came in another time when I was taking the class out for some activity and he didn't stay.

Instructor 1: Is this the general experience?

Students: Yes.

Student 1: He talked to the critic teacher and they did have conferences with each other.

Student 5: He never talked to my teacher. My teacher didn't even know him.

Student 1: Some of the instructors of the other seminars came.

Student 2: I was visited.

Instructor 2: What was the nature of the visit to you?

Student 2: It was more or less observation on the part of the campus instructor. He would come in and observe, and then, afterwards, he would ask me general questions pertaining to what was going on in the class, nothing really concrete. I felt if there were anything wrong, he would so state.

Student 1: He said if there were nothing wrong and if the class were running smoothly and if there were good control, then there was no need to stay.

Student 3: I had a little different experience. My coordinator never visited me, but my training teacher was new (this was her first time training anyone) so Dr. ——— did come in one day just to speak to her. While Dr. ——— was in there she observed me for about five minutes and then I was asked to go upstairs with her to talk about her observation of me. However, I couldn't see how in five minutes she could get such a widespread opinion of my teaching. She told me about all these flaws that were in my teaching. I knew this was not her opinion; this was my training teacher's opinion because she had stressed this all along. Therefore, I don't think anything beneficial came of this at all. I think if she stayed longer, but she didn't have the time, it would have been something different.

Instructor 2: I take it then that the contact between the student teacher and the campus during this nine-week period is relatively minimum.

Students: Yes. Unless we don't know about other meetings they might have.

Student 5: I imagine with the four laboratory schools the campus instructor is pressed for time, and regardless of the fact it is nine weeks, they still can't go to every place at once.

Instructor 2: Did you people find at the end of the day that the supervising teacher sat down and discussed the work that you had done?

Students: Yes.

Student 4: My teacher used to race me to the door.

Instructor 1: You didn't have any meetings?

Student 4: I had three conferences, one when I received my evaluation and two during the student-teaching period.

Instructor 2: What about the rest of you on this question?

Student 5: My teacher was very fair. She gave me a lot of time. During conferences she went over things I was weak in and where I could improve. I thought it was very beneficial.

Student 1: I found I never knew exactly where I stood in teaching. We had conferences every day for at least an hour. She would go over the points where I could improve and where she thought it would be beneficial to read up on something, but she would never say, "You did well in this." This, I had to assume myself.

Student 3: I think that you should be given some encouragement during teaching. I know I was constantly being knocked down and I just got so depressed I didn't know what I was doing after awhile.

Student 1: Until I received my evaluation, I didn't know how well I was doing.

Student 4: My teacher always told me I was doing well. I didn't know my faults until I received my evaluation. I would ask her and she would say everything is fine.

Student 2: I asked my teacher to evaluate me each day. She put down both the good and the bad points.

Student 5: I experienced the same thing. At least, I knew where I needed to improve.

Student 3: We also found that our master teachers often criticized us right in front of the children and we found that this created bedlam in some cases. It was actually harder for us to discipline the children after this experience.

The preceding reactions, which in our experience are quite typical of student reports, as well as our own observations during practice teaching periods, are the foundation for the following statements:

1. The criteria for the selection of a master or critic teacher are (when stated) vague, variable, and generally those of a single person, usually a principal. Because there is no reason to assume that the degree of agreement among principals as to what constitutes a "good" teacher is terribly high, it is not surprising that critic teachers vary enormously in numerous, important ways.

2. When a critic teacher is initially chosen she, of course, has never had experience or training in supervision. Training to a degree which could justifiably be dignified by the label "training" is never available to the critic teacher. Certainly such training is not required of the critic teacher.

3. Far more often than not, the critic teacher views the student teacher as a drill sergeant does the new recruits, that is, the student teacher must be given the rules and regulations of teaching so that the teaching routine is faithfully executed. The student teacher is told what to do, when to do it, and how to do it. It is small wonder that the student teacher, like the new recruits, frequently has hostile feelings toward the supervisor, guaranteeing a relationship not exactly conducive to productive learning.

4. The reverse of the previous point frequently occurs. The student is given minimal guidance or, so to speak, left to his own devices. Forcing the student to think for himself and to develop his own conceptions based on observation is, as a principle, not subject to criticism. However, when such a grant of independence does not reflect an understanding of the principles of learning on the part of the supervisor, there is consequently little or none of the kind of follow-through which makes for productive use of such independence; the student (particularly when he is not used to such independence) flounders, becomes more dependent, and learns little. Just as one cannot legislate attention in children (Chapter 3), one cannot legislate independence in the student teacher.

The practice-teaching period, like the internship in many other professions, is indispensable for the professional training of the teacher; as was seen in Chapter 2, no responsible critic of teacher training has advocated its elimination. It is surprising, therefore, that the practice-teaching experience has not received systematic study. There has been much discussion, for example, on when it should occur, how long it should be, and the need for it to be a truly stimulating experience. Even on the level of discussion, however, there has been little or no focus on the specific aims of the practice-teaching period, how such aims determine the nature of the student teacher–master teacher relationship, selection and training of the master teacher, and the crucial need for systematic study of what actually goes (or should go) on during this important phase of training.

In closing this chapter we would express the opinion that no problem area in education is as unstudied and as important as the practice-teaching period. What are desperately needed are studies which have as their aims a detailed description of what goes on between neophyte and supervisor, an explication of the principles which presumably underlie the ways in which this learning experience is structured and handled, the values implicit in these principles and their execution, the efficacy of the experiences which do or should precede practice teaching, and the development of procedures that would allow us to evaluate the effects of practice teaching on the neophyte teacher, procedures which would be better than private opinions.

6

Some Final Comments

This book has been concerned primarily with the implications of the point of view that the teacher, far from being a technician or imparter of knowledge, is an applier of psychological principles in a particular kind of learning situation. One of the major implications of this point of view is that improvement of the quality of teaching is not likely to take place in any marked kind of way by merely increasing the amount and variety of information which teachers should have.[1] Just as we must never confuse degree

[1] As we indicated in Chapter 2, we agree with those critics who have maintained that the liberal arts and science backgrounds of teachers have been far from adequate. However, in so agreeing, we do not assume that strengthening background in these areas will in any direct way increase teacher effectiveness—an assumption, by the way, which receives little or no support from research on transfer of training. Our agreement with the critics reflects the belief that the goals of teaching in our schools (elementary and high schools)—the attitudes toward learning and intellectual skills which we wish to engender in children —are outgrowths of the traditions and spirit of inquiry of the liberal arts and sciences. We hope that the greater one's background in these areas, the greater the appreciation of the values and modes of inquiry which have enabled these areas to expand man's knowledge, outlook, and skills. Until some evidence is forthcoming, however, we cannot assume that such appreciation increases in any marked kind of way, the skill of transmitting it in appropriate ways to children of different ages and capacities.

of education with degree of wisdom—the educated person is not necessarily "wise" in the sense that he can utilize or apply what he knows in appropriate, non-self-defeating ways—we must not confuse what a teacher knows with how she applies such knowledge.

A second major implication of our point of view is that the traditional ways in which teachers have been trained barely come to grips with the question of how one maximizes the possibility that a teacher's practice harmonizes with principles of learning and development. A symptom of this neglect is that educational psychology (as the psychology of learning) is viewed as something which has to do with how children learn and not with how teachers learn. The student in the process of becoming a teacher is not made acutely aware of how he is learning, that is, to utilize himself as a source of understanding of the nature of the learning process. We would advance the hypothesis that one of the major reasons so many teachers are dissatisfied with themselves in their work is that their training did not illuminate the nature of *their* learning process and how this relates to and affects the learning process of their pupils. They teach, but in the process they tend neither to give expression to their own experiences as a learner or to perceive the identity between themselves and their pupils. As a result, the teacher does tend to function as a technician who applies rules which are contradicted both by her own learning experiences and her pupils' unproductive learning. It is revealing, but not surprising, how many teachers can cogently criticize their professional preparation only to manifest these same shortcomings in their own practice. This is no different from what one frequently encounters in parent-child relationships: The parent resolves to rear his or her child to avoid the mistakes of which he was presumably the victim only to proceed in a way which brings about what he wanted to avoid. This analogy can be taken one step further: Many of these parents attempt to "legislate" a desirable characteristic in their child with the same unpredictable results as when a teacher legislates attention or motivation in her pupils by verbal command —a form of influence which we described and discussed in earlier chapters.

The point of view we have presented in this book cuts across many of the issues in today's raging controversy in education. Everyone is in favor of the learning process being guided in a way which results in productive learning, stimulates and maintains intellectual curiosity, and maximizes the utilization of the child's intellectual potential. However differently the proponents of various viewpoints in the controversy define such terms as "productive learning" and "intellectual curiosity," all would agree that they are utterly opposed to the sheer acquisition of knowledge. However much they may disagree on method and content, each would say that his goal is not only to have the child acquire knowledge, but also to think critically about it and utilize it appropriately in subsequent problem-solving. What many protagonists in the controversy have not done is to think through, in at least two respects, the implications of the judgment that the aim of learning is not merely to acquire knowledge. First, what are the implications of this judgment for how children are or should be taught, by which we mean a detailed description and examination of actual teaching situations exemplifying whatever may be considered proper or improper approaches to a goal we may agree is desirable or necessary? At the present time, we simply lack the kind of detailed description of "live" teaching by means of which we can gain a better understanding of what the different protagonists in the controversy actually mean and the degree to which their descriptions are consistent with stated aims. One can point to other fields where issues were greatly clarified and productive research initiated after systematic descriptions of the live situation became available for study. Until a great deal more of these kinds of systematic descriptions of classroom learning situations are forthcoming, it will be difficult to proceed to the scientific study of the issues involved.

A second implication (of the judgment that the aim of learning is not merely to acquire knowledge), which has not been thought through, is how to train teachers to guide the learning process so that agreed on aims are accomplished. Here, too, what is very much needed are detailed descriptions of how teachers are actually trained. We have had a surfeit of attractive course descriptions, unassailable statements of aims and hopes, and vague generalizations of what the future teacher is experiencing and learning in the course of training. What we need to know is not only to what the student is exposed, but the specifics of how it is structured, who structured it, and the role and perception of the student. Without detailed descriptions of what actually goes on between student and teacher and between student and master teacher, it is impossible to judge whether the theory (if there is one, and too frequently there is not) giving rise to training practices is adequately being reflected in how these practices are being implemented. What is so distressing to us is not only that the theory and practices of training frequently bear little relation to each other, but that neither bears a strong relationship to the reality of the everyday tasks of the teacher.

In Chapters 4 and 5 we endeavored to describe our views toward and practices in relation to teacher training. Although we do not view these chapters as models of description, we do hope and think that we have conveyed some idea of the kind of description which is needed.

Teacher training has not suffered from a lack of discussion. When we say, however, that teacher training is an unstudied problem, we mean that there has been a relative lack of effort to describe practices in a way to encourage the feeling that we know what they actually consist of, their relation to stated aims, and the problems we would encounter in scientifically testing the consequences of the training practices. We have said little or nothing in this book about the evaluation of training practices because we believe that this requires, as a first step, detailed descriptions which allow one to state specific assumptions and provide direction for the development of relevant techniques of evaluation. In addition, and in relation to the current education controversy, such descriptions should make the distinctions between different orientations to teacher training clearer and more amenable to that kind of research which would help shift the controversy from the realm of opinion to that of scientific inquiry.

References

Armstrong, W.E. The teacher education curriculum. *Journal of Teacher Education*, 1957, 8, 20-243.

Bain, A. *Education as a science*. New York: D. Appleton & Company, 1893.

Blau, J.L. John Dewey and American social thought. *Teachers College Record*, 1959, 61, 121-127.

Borrowman, M.L. *The liberal and technical in teacher education*. New York: Teachers College, Columbia University, 1956.

Brubacher, J.S. *The role of theory in professional status*. Swampscott, MA: New England Teacher Preparation Association, 1958.

Bruner, J.S. After John Dewey, what? *Saturday Review*, June, 1961, 44, 58-59.

Bruner, J.S. *The process of education*. Cambridge: Harvard University Press, 1961.

Crosby, O.A. The nation reaches a verdict in the case of people vs. today's schools. Reprinted in S.W. Scott and C.M. Hill, Eds., *Public education under criticism*. New York: Harper, 1954.

Davidson, K.S. & Sarason, S.B. Text anxiety and classroom observations. *Child Development*, 1961, 32, 199-210.

Dearborn, N.H. *The Oswego movement in American education*. New York: Teachers College, Columbia University, 1925.

Dewey, J. *The school and society*. Chicago: University of Chicago Press, 1900.

Dewey, J. *Democracy and education*. New York: Macmillan, 1916.

Dewey, J. *Experience and education*. New York: Macmillan, 1938.

Elsbree, W.S. *The American teacher*. New York: American Book Company, 1939.

Flexner, A. *The Flexner report on medical education in the United States and Canada in 1910*. Republished by Science and Health Publications, Inc., Suite 511, 1129 20th Street, Washington, D.C. 20036.

Griswold, A.W. *American educations' greatest need*. Saturday Review, March 14, 1959, 15-17.

Hanson, E.H. Viewpoints. *Education*, 1959, 79, 326-327.

Hilberry, C.B. Dedication and rededication. *Graduate Comment,* Wayne State University, 1961, IV, 5, 1.

Hulburd, D. *This happened in Pasadena.* New York: Macmillan, 1951.

Kelley, E.C. *Education for what is real.* New York: Harper, 1947.

Keppel, F. Master of arts in teaching. *Saturday Review,* 1961, June, 63-65.

Koerner, J.D. Basic education. *Education,* 1959, 79, 372-374.

Miller, R.I. Admiral Rickover on American education. *Journal of Teacher Education,* 1959, 10, 332- 357.

Payne, J. *Science and the act of education.* Boston: Educational Publishing Company, 1886.

Rickover, H.G. *Education and freedom.* New York: Dutton, 1959.

Rickover, H.G. Education in the U.S.S.R. and the U.S.A. *Graduate Comment,* Wayne State University, 1960, III, 3, 2-6.

Rugg, H. *The teacher of teachers.* New York: Harper, 1952.

Sarason, S.B., Davidson, K.S., Lighthall, F.F., Waite, R.R., & Ruebush, B.K. *Anxiety in elementary school children: A report of research.* New York: John Wiley and Sons, 1960.

Skaife, R.A. Conflicts can be solved. *Education,* 1958, 78, 387- 391.

Thomas, B. *Remarks to Chicago United Education Committee.* Chicago: Comprehensive Health Council, 108 N. State, #1201.